Everything But the Kitchen Sink

What Every Modern Woman Needs to Know

FRANCESCA BEAUMAN

illustrated by
Ben Cracknell

SSE

SIMON SPOTLIGHT ENTERTAINMENT
New York London Toronto Sydney

Excerpt from "The Beggar at the Manor" from *The Odyssey* by Homer, translated by Robert Fitzgerald. Copyright © 1961, 1963 by Robert Fitzgerald. Copyright renewed 1989 by Benedict R.C. Fitzgerald, on behalf of the Fitzgerald children. Reprinted by permission of Farrar, Straus and Giroux, LLC.

Extract from *Downhill all the Way* by Leonard Woolf reproduced by permission of the University of Sussex and the Society of Authors as the Literary Representative of the Estate of Leonard Woolf.

Diagram from the Stern Review reproduced under the terms of the Click-Use Licence.

Extract from *Forever Summer* by Nigella Lawson. Copyright © 2003 Nigella Lawson. Reprinted by permission of Hyperion. All rights reserved.

"Diamonds Are a Girl's Best Friend" Words by Leo Robin. Music by Jule Styne. Copyright © 1949 (Renewed) Consolidated Music Publishers Incorporated/Music Sales Corporation/Dorsey Brothers Music, USA. Dorsey Brothers Music Limited. Used by permission of Music Sales Limited. All Rights Reserved. International Copyright Secured.

Definition of "Rain" from Oxford English Dictionary (1989) edited by Simpson, J. & Weiner, E. By permission of Oxford University Press.

Quote from *Self-Consciousness* by John Updike reproduced by kind permission of John Updike.

Diagram based on Figure 1.1 in *Guns, Germs and Steel* by Jared Diamond reproduced by kind permission of Jared Diamond.

Extract from *Modern Manners* by Drusilla Beyfus reproduced by kind permission of Drusilla Beyfus.

Excerpt from *A Room of One's Own* by Virginia Woolf, copyright © 1929 by Harcourt, Inc. and renewed 1957 by Leonard Woolf, reprinted by permission of the publisher.

SSE

SIMON SPOTLIGHT ENTERTAINMENT
An imprint of Simon & Schuster Children's Publishing
1230 Avenue of the Americas, New York, New York 10020
Text copyright © 2007 by Francesca Beauman
Originally published as *The Woman's Book* in Great Britain in 2007 by Weidenfeld & Nicolson, an imprint of the Orion Publishing Group
First U.S. Edition 2007
All rights reserved, including the right of reproduction in whole or in part in any form.
SIMON SPOTLIGHT ENTERTAINMENT and related logo are trademarks of Simon & Schuster, Inc.
Designed by Jane Archer
Manufactured in the United States of America
First Edition 10 9 8 7 6 5 4 3 2 1
Library of Congress Cataloging-in-Publication Data
Beauman, Francesca.
Everything but the kitchen sink / by Francesca Beauman ; illustrated by Ben Cracknell.—1st ed.
p. cm.

ISBN 978-1-4516-5558-2

1. Curiosities and wonders. 2. Handbooks, vade-mecums, etc.
3. Women—Miscellanea. I. Cracknell, Ben. II. Title.
AG243.B415 2007
031.02—dc22
2007023534

Contents

Preface	*vii*
Everywoman	1
Useful Phrases	2
The Most Popular Girls' Names over the Past One Hundred Years	6
All Hail Vinegar	6
Women in Malawi	10
Winners of a "Best Actress" Oscar	11
Personal Advertisements	14
Ten Good Ideas	19
Getting Married	20
Mathematics	22
Voting	26
Bras	31
Group Sex	32
How to Buy a Bathing Suit	36
Memorable Film Lines of the 1930s Through the 1970s	38
The Personality of a Beehive	40

In Case of a Genuine Emergency   43

Chocolate   47

The Terminology of Sleeves   48

How to Clean a Pearl Necklace   53

Pets   54

Drink Myths   58

Cardiopulmonary Resuscitation   60

Martinis   61

The Blues   63

Low Spirits   67

Cars   68

Carbon Emissions (or, How to Murder One's Grandchildren)   73

How to Drive in Snow   77

Ballet   78

The Global AIDS Epidemic   83

How to Eat a Pineapple   89

What to Drink When   93

How to Put Up a Tent in the Dark   95

The Constellations   97

Major Foreign Aid Donors   103

New Year's Eve   104

Tattoos   106

Shoes 109

Animal Stings, Bites, or Otherwise
Unfriendly Approaches 112

The Approximate Caloric Value of
Various Foodstuffs 118

Nobel Peace Prize Winners 119

Placing a Bet at the Horse Races 124

What to Cook for a "Wild" Dinner Party 128

What to Cook for a Slightly Less "Wild"
Dinner Party 129

A Selection of the World's Largest
Cut Diamonds 130

Homeopathy 135

Therapy 137

The Thank-You Letter 141

How to Make an Abode Gemütlich in Just
Three-quarters of an Hour (or, "A Daffodil
in a Glass Jar") 143

Rain 145

Diets 148

How Humans Spread 152

The Drinks Party 152

The Muses 159

How to Deliver a Baby 160

How to Use a Compass 161

A Few World War II Heroines 163

Long–Term Investing 171

Sailing 174

The Window Box 177

Philosophy 183

Toward Helen of Troy 188

How to Get Rid of Guests at the End of a
Dinner Party 190

American Literature over the Past Three
Hundred and Fifty Years 191

The Origin of "Woman" 196

Preface

The first preface ever to be published in North America appeared in 1640 in *The Bay Psalm Book*. It was written by Robert Mather, and addressed the issue of whether or not it was acceptable to sing in church.

Remember this.

For although one can never know quite when the above information will be useful, the fact is, it will. Rarely in history has more been demanded of our sex. Women at the beginning of the twenty-first century are widely expected to be able to carry on a conversation about the political instability in Chechnya, wrestle an alligator to the ground, and clean a pearl necklace—ideally, all at the same time. So while it used to be the likes of Emily Post who merrily dispensed advice to the ladies of the age, today a new kind of manual is required—a manual that addresses not just issues of etiquette, but also the many and varied cultural reference points that currently constitute a woman's everyday existence.

This is that manual.

In essence, it concerns matters of right and wrong (as all the best books do): the right way to plant a window box or to get rid of guests at a dinner party, the wrong way to have a tattoo or to shelter from a nuclear attack. Thus the words "maybe," "perhaps," and "probably" simply do not feature here.

Read one entry while you eat your breakfast

cereal, browse through another while you wait for your Tres Santos Colombia Almaguer to brew. Read up on carbon emissions as you stand in line at the grocery store, and wonder at the history of personal ads while your nail polish dries. When on hold with the cable company, remind yourself whether or not it is necessary to write a thank-you letter following an evening of group sex.

Keep this tome in your backpack or your Birkin bag, in the basket of your bicycle or in the champagne fridge in your limousine. Who knows when you might next need to rescue yourself from a particularly intractable conversational conundrum . . . ?

FRANCESCA BEAUMAN
LONDON, UK
2007

Everything
But the
Kitchen Sink

Everywoman

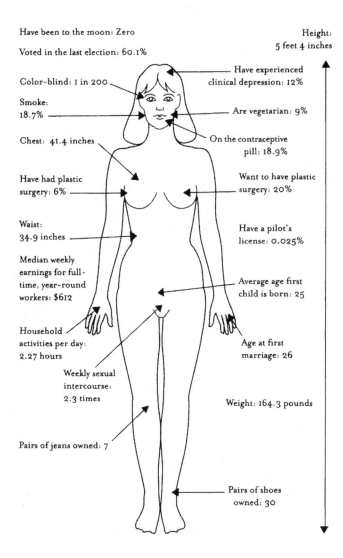

Have been to the moon: Zero

Voted in the last election: 60.1%

Color-blind: 1 in 200

Smoke: 18.7%

Chest: 41.4 inches

Have had plastic surgery: 6%

Waist: 34.9 inches

Median weekly earnings for full-time, year-round workers: $612

Household activities per day: 2.27 hours

Weekly sexual intercourse: 2.3 times

Pairs of jeans owned: 7

Height: 5 feet 4 inches

Have experienced clinical depression: 12%

Are vegetarian: 9%

On the contraceptive pill: 18.9%

Want to have plastic surgery: 20%

Have a pilot's license: 0.025%

Average age first child is born: 25

Age at first marriage: 26

Weight: 164.3 pounds

Pairs of shoes owned: 30

Useful Phrases

ENGLISH	Hello	Please	Thank you
DANISH	Davs	Vær venlig	Tak
DUTCH	Hallo	Alsjeblieft	Dank je wel
FRENCH	Bonjour	S'il vous plaît	Merci
GERMAN	Hallo	Bitte	Danke
GREEK	Geia sas	Parakalo	Efharisto
ITALIAN	Ciao	Per favore	Grazie
PORTUGUESE	Alô!	Por favor	Obrigado!
BRAZILIAN PORTUGUESE	Oi	Por favor	Obrigado/a
RUSSIAN	Zdrastvooytye	Pazhalsta	Spaseeba

Would you like to dance?	Wow, you're gorgeous! Yes please, I'd love to.	No, thank you. Please leave me alone.
Vil du danse med mig?	Wow, du er gorgeous! Ja, behage, jeg ville elske hen til.	Ikke, tak for lån. Lad mig være i fred.
Heb je zin om te dansen?	Wouw, wat ben je mooi! Ja, graag. Dat lijkt me erg leuk.	Nee, dank je wel. Laat me alsjeblieft met rust.
Voudriez-vous danser avec moi?	Hou la, vous êtes splendides! Oui s'il vous plait, j'aimerais à danser.	Non, merci. Laissez-moi tranquille.
Möchten sie mit mir tanzen?	Wow, sie sind wundervoll! Ja, bitte, ja das wuerde ich sehr gerne.	Nein, danke. Bitte lassen sie mich in ruhe.
Theleis na xorepsoume?	Wow, ise panemorfos. Ne, efharisto, tha eithela ply.	Oxi, efharisto. Afisteme isihi parakalo.
Vuoi ballare con me?	Lei è magnifico! Sì per favore, amerei a.	No, grazie. Mi lasci in pace.
Você quer dançar?	Wow, você é magnífico! Sim por favor, amaria a.	Não, obrigado. Deixa-me em paz.
Quer dançar comigo?	Nossa, você é lindo! Sim, adoraria.	Não, obrigado. Eu não quero nada com você, sai pra lá.
Khateetye paytee patantsevat.	Ti preekrasna vigleedeesh. Da, pazhalsta, ya s oodavol stveeyem.	Nyet, spaseeba. Astaf'tye meenya f pakoye pazhalsta.

ENGLISH	Hello	Please	Thank you
POLISH	Cześć	Proszę	Dziękuję
SPANISH	Hola	Por favor	Gracias
SWEDISH	hej	Varsågod	tack så mycket
CHINESE (MANDARIN)	Nee hao	Ching	Shie-shie
KOREAN	An-nyong haseyo	Pootak-ham-needa	Kamsa-ham-needa
JAPANESE	Konnichiwa	Kudasai	Arigato
ARABIC	Ahlan	Min fadlak	Shukran
HEBREW	Shalom	Bevakasha	Toda
AFRIKAANS	Hallo	Asseblief	Dankie
ICELANDIC	Halló	Takk	Nei takk
TURKISH	Cehennem	Mutlu etmek	Eyvallah

Would you like to dance?	Wow, you're gorgeous! Yes please, I'd love to.	No, thank you. Please leave me alone.
Czy chcialbyś zatańczyć?	O kurcze, jestés boski! Pewnie, że chce.	Nie, dziękuję. Proszę mnie zostawić w spokoju.
¿Quisiera bailar conmigo?	Caramba! Estas muy lindo! Si, vamos.	No, gracias. ¡Déjeme en paz!
Skulle du vilja dansa?	Wow, du är underbar! Ja tack! Jag vill gärna.	Nej tack, lämna mig ifred.
Ni yao bu yao jen wo tiaowu?	Nee jen piao-liarng! Dwee, ching, wo yee-ding lai.	Boo-dwee, shie-shie. Ching nee dso ba.
Choom-choo ro kaseege-ssumneekka?	Motjeem-needa. Ne, pootak-ham-needa, chaw-ssumneeda.	A-neeyo, kamsa-ham-needa. Hawa-ja eetge he-jooseep-seeaw.
Isshoni odorimasenka?	Sugoy! Hai, kudasai, zehi tomo.	Ie, kekko des, hitori shite oyte kudasai.
Hal tuhibb an tarqus?	Shaklak Hilw! Naahm, min fadlak. Sa-yusharrifnee.	Laa, shukran. Utruknee wahdee, lau samaht.
Ha'im tirtsi lircod iti?	Ata nie-e nifla! Ken, bevakasha, beratzon.	Lo, toda. Azov oti bevakasha.
Sal jy met my dans?	Sjoe maar jy is oulik! Ja, dankie dit sal lekker wees.	Nee dankie, los my uit.
Viltu dansa við mig?	Vá, þú ert yndisfagur! Já, þóknast, eg myndi gjarnan.	Neitun, pakka pu. Lattu mig i fridi.
Dans etmek ile beni?	Vay, sen are çok güzel! Evet, mutlu etmek, i almak senin davet.	Hayır, eyvallah. ayrılmak beni tek başına.

5

The Most Popular Girls' Names over the Past One Hundred Years

	1905	1935	1965	1995	2005
1st	Mary	Mary	Lisa	Jessica[1]	Emily
2nd	Helen	Shirley[2]	Mary	Ashley	Emma
3rd	Margaret	Barbara	Karen	Emily	Madison
4th	Anna	Betty[3]	Kimberley	Samantha	Abigail
5th	Ruth	Patricia	Susan	Sarah	Olivia

All Hail Vinegar

Dancer Margot Fonteyn defined magic as "genius." To playwright and poet Ntozake Shange, magic was "woman." To others—the clever ones—magic is vinegar. The use of vinegar for a range of household chores sounds like the sort of instruction that one's grandmother submitted to during wartime only because she had no other choice. Fiddlesticks to that. In fact, it actually works—brilliantly, and without making the whole house reek of the stuff. It is also a hundred times cheaper and a million times more eco-friendly than most commercial products.

---

1   Jessica is originally a Hebrew name from the Old Testament meaning "He sees," "God's grace," or "wealthy." It was first used in its current form by William Shakespeare in *The Merchant of Venice* for the daughter of a Jewish merchant.

2   The increased popularity of the name "Shirley" in the 1930s was due to child star Shirley Temple. The cocktail of the same name was invented for her by a barman at Chasen's in Beverly Hills and is a mixture of ginger ale, grenadine syrup, and orange juice decorated with a maraschino cherry and slice of lemon—so also an excellent option for those who are pregnant and/or on the wagon.

3   Famous Bettys include Betty Grable, Betty White, Betty Smith, Betty Friedan, Betty Ford, Betty Buckley, and Betty Crocker—an invented persona rather than a real person, but an essential cultural reference point nonetheless.

USES

(Unless otherwise stated, distilled white vinegar is advised for cleaning, and apple cider vinegar for health and beauty. Pour it into a spray bottle first to make it easier to use.)

• **Window cleaner.** Dilute with four parts water.

• **Fabric softener.** Add about half a cup to the wash, just as one would with conventional fabric softener.

• **Air freshener.** Mix together 2 tablespoons of vinegar, 2 cups of water, and a teaspoon of baking soda (another magic creation). Do not be alarmed when it foams a little—this will not last long. Then spray the concoction liberally around the house. Alternatively, pour it into a bowl and leave it lying around—that is, as long as you are not worried that guests might mistake it for dog pee.

• **Stain remover.** Mix together vinegar and water in equal parts, then spray it on the stain in question, just as one would with conventional stain remover, before you put the garment in the washing machine.

• **Weed killer.** Pour straight onto the weedy patch. It sometimes needs a couple of applications.

• **Toilet cleaner.** Pour in, then leave overnight.

• **Treatment for stings.** Especially if stung by a jellyfish (see page 114).

• **Drain cleaner.** Pour in, then leave overnight, both to remove smells and unclog (small) blockages.

• **Wallpaper remover.** Once the top layer of wallpaper has been removed, spray on some vinegar and leave it for a couple of minutes. The backing should then pull away relatively easily. Scrape the excess glue off the wall, wipe the remaining glue away with vinegar, then rinse with water.

- **Lice remover.** Dip a comb in vinegar, then go to work on the hair as usual. It works by helping to break down the glue that the parasites use to cling on. Incidentally, it will also give the hair a welcome shininess by neutralizing the alkali consistency of most shampoos.

- **Grease cutter.** Use straight vinegar to clean the oven, stovetop, or grill. Spray on, leave for a few minutes, then wipe off.

- **Treatment for sunburn.** Soak a towel in a mixture of half vinegar and half water. It may sting a little at first, but it will eventually ease the pain and prevent blistering. The result is worth it. This also works with other types of mild burns.

- **Furniture polish.** Mix together equal parts of vinegar and vegetable oil, then apply with a soft cloth.

- **Lime deposits remover.** Soak a paper towel in vinegar, then use an elastic band to secure it over the area to be treated. Left overnight, the film will be easy to wipe away in the morning. This sometimes works even more effectively when the vinegar is boiled first.

- **Inside-the-ear cleaner.** Mix together one third vinegar, one third water, and one third rubbing alcohol, then pour it into a (clean) dropper bottle for use whenever. A couple of minutes after application, the ear should be cleaned with a tissue. The technique also works on cats and dogs to prevent ear infections.

- **Insect repellent.** Just spray. It works on all kinds of insects. Ticks particularly hate it. Try pouring vinegar down any openings that ants find to sneak into the house—they will soon find some other, more hospitable home to visit. One's horse may also benefit—add five teaspoons of the cider kind to the horse's oats every morning and evening to reduce fly bites.

- **Odor remover.** Spray on a dog to remove the smell of skunk.

- **Animal coat enhancer.** Mix together half a cup of vinegar with about two pints of water, then spray onto a horse or a dog to make its coat gleam. It also helps prevent infections.

- **Glue solvent.** Apply vinegar to the area, leaving it to soak until results are seen. Be warned, though—this might take a while.

- **In red cabbage.** Much underrated. (See page 130 for the recipe.) Even those who claim not to like cabbage like this dish—even if they don't know it yet. Especially successful at Christmastime.

- **Brass cleaner.** Mix together one part vinegar with ten parts water, then soak brass as necessary.

- **Treatment for alopecia.** Pour vinegar on the head, then wrap in a hot towel and leave overnight. Repeat every night until some improvement.

- **Rust remover.** Soak the offending article in a bowl of vinegar for as long as necessary. (This works better on bolts than on cars. . . .)

- **Denture cleaner.** Soak dentures in vinegar for about

half an hour or as long as one would with commercial denture cleaner, then brush thoroughly.

- **Fish tank cleaner.** Soak a cloth in vinegar, then wipe all the way around the inside of the tank where white mineral deposits tend to accumulate. Be assured that the vinegar is harmless to fish.

- **French fry enhancer.** Pour liberally, ideally when drunk.

Magic indeed.

Women in Malawi

	MALAWI	U.S.
Total female population	6,621,100	152,938,800
Life expectancy	40	80
Female literacy	54%	99%
Percentage of women over 15 with HIV	7.6%	0.12%
Average age of women at first marriage	19	26
Women who use contraception	30.6%	76.4%
Annual number of deaths in childbirth per 100,000	1,800	17
Average number of children per woman	6.1	2.0
Percentage of girls attending primary school	99%	98%
Percentage of girls attending secondary school	23%	98%
Maternity leave	8 weeks at 100% full pay	12 weeks at 0% full pay
Female members of parliament	14%	25%

Source: United Nations Statistics Division

Winners of a "Best Actress" Oscar

1927–28	Janet Gaynor	*Seventh Heaven*
1928–29	Mary Pickford	*Coquette*
1929–30	Norma Shearer	*The Divorcee*
1930–31	Marie Dressler	*Min and Bill*
1931–32	Helen Hayes	*The Sin of Madelon Claudet*
1932–33	Katharine Hepburn	*Morning Glory*
1934	Claudette Colbert	*It Happened One Night*
1935	Bette Davis	*Dangerous*[1]
1936	Luise Rainer	*The Great Ziegfeld*
1937	Luise Rainer	*The Good Earth*
1938	Bette Davis	*Jezebel*
1939	Vivien Leigh	*Gone with the Wind*
1940	Ginger Rogers	*Kitty Foyle*
1941	Joan Fontaine	*Suspicion*
1942	Greer Garson	*Mrs. Miniver*[2]
1943	Jennifer Jones	*The Song of Bernadette*
1944	Ingrid Bergman	*Gaslight*
1945	Joan Crawford	*Mildred Pierce*
1946	Olivia de Havilland	*To Each His Own*
1947	Loretta Young	*The Farmer's Daughter*
1948	Jane Wyman	*Johnny Belinda*
1949	Olivia de Havilland	*The Heiress*

---

1 "An actor is something less than a man; an actress is more than a woman" read the inscription on Bette Davis's cigarette case.

2 Greer Garson's win holds the record for the longest acceptance speech ever given at an Academy Awards ceremony. It lasted approximately seven minutes.

1950	Judy Holliday	*Born Yesterday*
1951	Vivien Leigh	*A Streetcar Named Desire*
1952	Shirley Booth	*Come Back, Little Sheba*
1953	Audrey Hepburn	*Roman Holiday*
1954	Grace Kelly	*The Country Girl*
1955	Anna Magnani	*The Rose Tattoo*
1956	Ingrid Bergman	*Anastasia*
1957	Joanne Woodward	*The Three Faces of Eve*
1958	Susan Hayward	*I Want To Live!*
1959	Simone Signoret	*Room at the Top*
1960	Elizabeth Taylor	*Butterfield 8*
1961	Sophia Loren	*Two Women*
1962	Anne Bancroft	*The Miracle Worker*
1963	Patricia Neal	*Hud*
1964	Julie Andrews	*Mary Poppins*
1965	Julie Christie	*Darling*
1966	Elizabeth Taylor	*Who's Afraid of Virginia Woolf?*
1967	Katharine Hepburn	*Guess Who's Coming to Dinner?*
1968	Katharine Hepburn; Barbra Streisand (tie)	*The Lion in Winter; Funny Girl*[3]
1969	Maggie Smith	*The Prime of Miss Jean Brodie*
1970	Glenda Jackson	*Women In Love*
1971	Jane Fonda	*Klute*
1972	Liza Minnelli	*Cabaret*
1973	Glenda Jackson	*A Touch of Class*

3   The two actresses received 3,030 votes each—the only exact tie in the history of the Oscars.

1974	Ellen Burstyn	*Alice Doesn't Live Here Anymore*
1975	Louise Fletcher	*One Flew Over the Cuckoo's Nest*
1976	Faye Dunaway	*Network*
1977	Diane Keaton	*Annie Hall*
1978	Jane Fonda	*Coming Home*
1979	Sally Field	*Norma Rae*
1980	Sissy Spacek	*Coal Miner's Daughter*
1981	Katharine Hepburn	*On Golden Pond*
1982	Meryl Streep	*Sophie's Choice*
1983	Shirley MacLaine	*Terms of Endearment*
1984	Sally Field	*Places in the Heart*
1985	Geraldine Page	*The Trip to Bountiful*[4]
1986	Marlee Matlin	*Children of a Lesser God*
1987	Cher	*Moonstruck*
1988	Jodie Foster	*The Accused*
1989	Jessica Tandy	*Driving Miss Daisy*
1990	Kathy Bates	*Misery*
1991	Jodie Foster	*The Silence of the Lambs*
1992	Emma Thompson	*Howards End*
1993	Holly Hunter	*The Piano*
1994	Jessica Lange	*Blue Sky*
1995	Susan Sarandon	*Dead Man Walking*

---

4   Geraldine Page was so surprised when it was announced that she had won the award for Best Actress that before she went up on stage to receive it, she had to scrabble around for a while to find her shoes, which she had kicked off underneath her seat.

1996	Frances McDormand[5]	*Fargo*
1997	Helen Hunt	*As Good As It Gets*
1998	Gwyneth Paltrow	*Shakespeare in Love*
1999	Hilary Swank	*Boys Don't Cry*
2000	Julia Roberts	*Erin Brockovich*
2001	Halle Berry	*Monster's Ball*
2002	Nicole Kidman	*The Hours*
2003	Charlize Theron	*Monster*
2004	Hilary Swank	*Million Dollar Baby*
2005	Reese Witherspoon	*Walk the Line*
2006	Helen Mirren	*The Queen*

Personal Advertisements

In July 1695, alongside the advertisements for a cobbler's apprentice, an Arabian stallion, and a secondhand bed that appeared on page three of the popular London weekly pamphlet *A Collection for Improvement of Husbandry and Trade*, the first-ever personal advertisement was published:

> *A Gentleman about 30 Years of Age, that says he had a Very Good Estate, would willingly Match himself to some Good Young Gentlewoman, that has a Fortune of 3000l. or thereabouts, and he will make Settlement to Content.*

Henceforth, the personals were to become a significant player in the history of courtship.

---

5 Frances McDormand was the first person to win for a film directed by a spouse (Joel Coen), though others have been similarly nominated: Gena Rowlands for *A Woman Under the Influence* (directed by husband John Cassavetes). Melina Mercouri for *Never on Sunday* (directed by husband Jules Dassin) and Julie Andrews for *Victor/Victoria* (directed by husband Blake Edwards).

A Single gentleman, between 30 and 40, whose character shall bear the strictest enquiry, would think himself happy to enter into the marriage-state with an agreeable lady, of a moderate fortune: he hopes the fair sex will excuse this public method of addressing them, as his application to business prevents any other means; and he knows there are many amiable ladies, who, by a retired life, are hid from the day world; to these he addresses himself: it is a companion and a friend for life he wants, and regards not so much the outward ornaments of beauty and elegance, as the purity of the mind. Any lady who will answer this advertisement by a line directed to Y.Z. at No. 30, Cow-lane, West Smithfield, may depend upon the strictest honour and secrecy.

—Daily Gazette, 1771

MATRIMONY. A Gentleman of very considerable fortune, about the age of forty, offers himself as an Husband to any well-educated, amiable and agreeable Lady, of good character and not more than thirty years of age, and as much younger as may be, who will undertake to exercise those attentions which his particular situation requires. Though he possesses an excellent and unimpaired constitution, he is afflicted with an incurable weakness in his knees, occasioned by the kick of an Ostrich, in the East Indies, which disables him from walking, rising from his chair, or getting from his bed, without assistance. That assistance he wishes to receive from the tender care of an affectionate young Lady. Fortune is not an object of his consideration.

Letters address to M.P. at Mr. Wallis's, Printseller, Ludgate-street, will receive every proper attention.

—The Times, 1786

MATRIMONY. A Lady, about 25 years of age, who has been flattered with the idea of possessing an agreeable person, and who, without any flattery at all, is in the actual possession of an independent fortune, solicits the attention of any young gentleman of birth, education, and personal consequence. The ill usage of her relations has obliged her to separate herself from them; and they, in revenge, not only employ their utmost malice to disturb her repose, but threaten prosecutions to deprive her of her fortune. Any such Gentleman, therefore, who will stand forth as her protector, to save her from the tyranny of her family on the one hand, and the impositions of lawyers on the other, shall be rewarded with the object he has protected and the fortune he has preserved. Letters addressed for Eleanora, at Mr. Materius's, Charing-cross, will have due attention.

—The Times, 1788

An agreeable and accomplished Woman would be glad to engage herself with a Single Gentleman. The reason of this public application is that the Lady is almost a stranger in this metropolis. A line addressed to X.I.F. to be left at the office of this Paper, will be answered immediately.

—Morning Chronicle, 1789

I, John Hobnall, am at this writing five and forty, a widower, and in

15

want of a wife. I have a good cottage with a couple of acres of land, for which I pay £2 a year. I have five children, four of them old enough to be in employment, three sides of bacon, and some pigs ready for market. I should like to have a woman fit to take care of her house when I am out . . . A good sterling woman would be preferred, who would take care of the pigs.

—Blackwood, 1837

The advertiser, who has been much abroad, has no relations, feels lonely, and possesses a good round sum for the matrimonial cash-box, wishes to find a single or widow lady in a similar position, having a wish to marry. As to personal attractions, an interview is best to satisfy. He is genteel, of studious habits, gentle temper, neat in dress, and fond of travelling. Not exact as to age. Would prefer a plain, neat lady, rather than a dashy person. . . . Address to R. Daron, 193 Bishopsgate-street Without, London

—News of the World, 1851

A young lady, disgusted with fortune hunters and insincere friends, is anxious to engage in a correspondence with some young gentleman who will give her a true, manly Heart in exchange for a fortune and a wife. Any gentleman matrimonially inclined may address Miss Fannie De F. Le S., Poughkeepsie, NY

—New York Herald, 1857

The young woman in a dark green bonnet who, on Wednesday last, in the Bleecker Street omnibus, about the corner of Broome Street, tripped over the foot of the gentleman in nankeen trowsers, is earnestly requested to communicate her address to Eugene, Union Square P.O. N.B. *Cartes de visite* exchanged.

—New York Herald, 1865

Wanted—by a young lady, aged nineteen, of pleasing countenance, good figure, agreeable manners, general information and varied accomplishments. who has studied every thing, from the Creation to crochet, a situation in the family of a gentleman. She will take the head of the table, manage his household, scold his servants, nurse his babies (when they arrive), check his tradesmen's bills, accompany him to the theatre, cut the leaves of his new book, sew on his buttons, warm his slippers, and generally make his life happy. Apply in the first place, by letter, to Louisa Caroline, Linden Grove, London, and afterward to Papa, upon the premises.

—The Times, 1873

Lilian, Gladys and Rosalie, daughters of a deceased officer, have good incomes, ages 22, 20 and 18, don't want to die old maids . . .

—Matrimonial News, 1885

The young and highly accomplished daughter of an American millionaire desires to contract an early aristocratic marriage . . . A title (English if possible) is preferred, but is not essential. Means a secondary consideration, but ancestry a sine qua non. Ample settlements.

—Marriage Gazette, 1895

In more recent times, it has become entirely acceptable to meet someone via a personal advertisement, either in a newspaper or on the Internet. Anyone who thinks otherwise is not only wrong, but also stupid. It is an essential tool in the modern courtship process, and not to be mocked.

INTERNET COURTSHIP

To ease the inevitable awkwardness of a first attempt at courtship over the Internet, there are a few guidelines to follow. Do not be daunted by the number of websites that exist to facilitate the process; however, it is important to weigh the options carefully. Just as the type of bar one goes to dictates the type of man one is likely to meet, so too does the type of website. To meet a thirty-five-year-old man who works in the media or the public sector and who also happens to be vegetarian, go to www.greensingles.com. To meet a fifty-five-year-old man who is a professor or journalist, try the website of the New York Review of Books (www.nybooks.com/classifieds/#personals). Simply to cast the net as wide as possible, go to www.eharmony.com or www.match.com, two of the largest Internet dating sites in the country.

Be circumspect when composing or responding to an ad. A recent study revealed that what people look for relates closely to men's and women's evolutionary instincts.

Women's preferences:	Men's preferences:
1. **Commitment**	1. **Attractiveness**
2. **Social skills**	2. **Commitment**
3. **Resources**	3. **Social skills**
4. **Attractiveness**	4. **Resources**

It is important to be sufficiently broad-minded in terms of demands made early on. Placing an advertisement in which a dislike is professed for "short men," "men with glasses," or "men with small hands" reveals oneself as the sort of person who treats men like made-to-measure curtains. This is to be avoided. There is no way of predicting who one is going to fall in love with, and a huge number of people end up rather surprising themselves with their ultimate choice of partner; thus, it is foolish to narrow down the options too soon.

Once a potential match surfaces, exchange photographs as soon as possible. Do not tell too many lies. E-mail each other for a sufficient length of time before arranging to meet; this avoids too many ghastly surprises when you finally do. It also ensures that there is at least one topic of conversation with which to open proceedings—"How did that meeting go?" or "Did you manage to find your sister a birthday present?" for example. Also, be polite: stay for two drinks at least. Refrain from making phone calls to girlfriends when you go to the ladies' room. Finally, in terms of what to wear . . . when in doubt, overdress. This applies generally, in fact.

Personal advertisement abbreviations

LTR: long term relationship

GSOH: good sense of humor

WLTM: would like to meet

N/S: nonsmoker

S/A: straight acting

ALAWP: all letters answered with photo

ND: nondrinker

OHAC: own house and car

BDSM: bondage, domination, sadism, and masochism

W/E: well-endowed

MBA: married but available

VGL: very good looking (not to be confused with VPL: visible panty line)

NSA: no strings attached

TDH: tall, dark, and handsome

WTR: willing to relocate

As Nancy Mitford put it so succinctly in *The Pursuit of Love*: "Wooing, so tiring."

Ten Good Ideas

Flush toilet	1589	Sir John Harington	England
Braille	1829	Louis Braille	France
Safety pin	1849	Walter Hunt	U.S.A.
Paper clip	1900	Johann Waaler	Norway
Frozen food	1923	Clarence Birdseye	U.S.A.
Launderette	1934	J. F. Cantrell	U.S.A.
Mobile phone	1947	Richard Frenkiel and Joel Engel of Bell Labs	U.S.A.[1]
Contact lenses	1948	Kevin Tuohy	U.S.A.
The Pill	1954	Gregory Pincus and John Rock	U.S.A.
Post-it note	1980	Art Fry of 3M	U.S.A.

---

1 It is open to debate whether the mobile phone fits into this category; many might argue otherwise.

Getting Married

Alice laughed: "There's no use trying," she said; "one can't believe impossible things."

"I daresay you haven't had much practice," said the Queen. "When I was younger, I always did it for half an hour a day. Why, sometimes I've believed as many as six impossible things before breakfast."'

—*Lewis Carroll*, Alice Through the
Looking Glass (1872)

It is a well-known statistic that approximately half of all marriages end in divorce. Yet despite this, 2004 saw 2,279,00 such leaps of faith take place. Marriage, it seems, is an institution that refuses to die out.

HOW TO KNOW WHETHER OR NOT TO ACCEPT A PROPOSAL OF MARRIAGE

In the modern world, simply being in love is not enough to make a relationship work. It is not even close to being enough, in fact. A host of other factors are involved, the most important of which is *timing*. This is depressing, unromantic even, but true. When it comes to marriage, it is especially true. The most eloquent proponent of this theory is that great commentator on modern times, *Sex and the City*'s Carrie Bradshaw. In her view, men are like taxis. They drive around all day picking up women; then, one day, their light goes on all of a sudden, and *boom!* They are ready to get married, and will simply marry the first woman who crosses their path thereafter whom they find at least vaguely acceptable.

To this end, a simple mathematical formula exists to help one ascertain whether or not to accept a proposal of marriage.

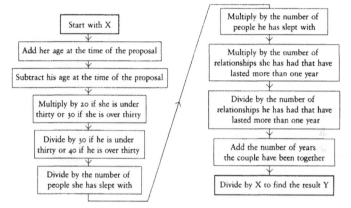

If Y > 0 but < 1, the couple should get married.

If Y < 0 or Y > 1, the couple should not get married.

(Some leeway exists either way; so if Y = 1.5, for example, that is acceptable.)

If Y = 0 exactly, however, the couple should definitely not get married, for revealed in this is the fact that at least one of the participants has either not had sex with anyone else but his or her intended or has not had a long-term relationship with anyone else but his or her intended. In the age we live in, either scenario augers disaster in all but the most exceptional of couples.

AVERAGE COST OF A WEDDING

	$	%
Outfits for the bride and the groom	2,606	9
Ceremony	2,525	8
Favors and gifts	1,121	3
Flowers	1,969	7
Rings	2,066	7
Music	953	3
Photography	3,688	12
Reception	14,169	47
Stationery	847	3
Transportation	410	1
Total	**30,354**	**100**

Throughout the process, try to be guided by double Nobel Prize–winning scientist Marie Curie. In July 1895 she wore a simple navy blue suit when she married Pierre Curie. She then wore this same suit to work in the laboratory every day for a decade or so—after all, the color did not show the stains too much. This refusal to submit to the silliness of some of life's rituals expresses a way of looking at the world that is to be much admired and, as far as possible, emulated.

Mathematics

"Sir Isaac Newton, though so deep in algebra and fluxions, could not readily make up a common account: and, when he was Master of the Mint, used to get somebody to make up his accounts for him." So claimed Alexander Pope (1688–1744), the implication being that every one of us has our limitations. For many, mathematics is one of them. There is no doubt that much of the calculus, trigonometry, and the like that one learns at school is limited in its usefulness, but other elements of mathematics are decidedly not. Yes, yes, one knows how to perform these mental machinations *in theory*—but in the heat of the moment, as one fights one's way down the escalator at the Crate & Barrel sale, how many of us are really so confident?

I. PERCENTAGES

The fraction method
How much of a reduction is 75% off an $80 Crate & Barrel toaster?

Turn the 75% into a fraction—3/4. To work out what 3/4 of $80 is, first work out what 1/4 is (divide 80 by 4 to get to 20), then multiply this by 3.

The result? A reduction of $60. And a bargain.

The decimal method
If one invites 150 people to one's birthday party, how many are likely to decline the invitation, given that the average percentage of people to decline invitations of this sort is approximately 30%?

Turn 30% into a decimal—0.3. Then multiply 150 by 0.3.

Alternatively, cheat by first working out 10% of 150—which is 15—then multiplying the resulting figure by 3.

The result? 45 people are likely to decline.

2. PROBABILITY

Probability is calculated as the number of successful outcomes divided by the total number of possible outcomes. Thus, when playing craps at a Las Vegas casino at three in the morning in a sparkly frock, let it be known that the odds are as follows when two dice are thrown at the same time:

Total of the two dice	Odds against in a single toss
2	35 to 1
3	17 to 1
4	11 to 1
5	8 to 1
6	6.2 to 1
7	5 to 1
8	6.2 to 1
9	8 to 1
10	11 to 1
11	17 to 1
12	35 to 1

3. VOLUME

Just as the area of dance floor required to create a makeshift disco in one's very own home is calculated by multiplying the length of the room by the width of the room, similarly the volume of water required to fill the pond in the back garden enough to keep the koi content is calculated by multiplying pond length by its width by its depth. The result is measured in cubic centimeters or meters. The volume of an irregular-shaped object, such as a jug to be filled with sangria on a breezy summer's day, is much more complicated. Take the length of the object, and call that x, then take the area of a cross section of the object taken perpendicular to the length. Find out how the area of the cross section varies as a function of its distance along x, and call that f(x). Finally, take the integral of f(x) as x varies from 0 to the length of the object—by which time one rather deserves the whole pitcher to oneself, quite frankly.

4. LONG DIVISION

Say the conundrum is how to divide a restaurant bill of $636 among twelve people (such a trial, and a mandate in itself against never going out to dinner in groups of more than six). A number of cheat methods should be attempted before a calculator on a cell phone is produced (a terrible admission that one's brain is not quite as agile as it perhaps once was). Realistically, though, for a more complex sum this may well be the only option—in which case, at least keep the telephone under the table.

First, estimate a rough answer: 636 ÷ 12 is close to 600 ÷ 12, which is the same as 60 ÷ 12, plus a 0, i.e., 50—plus a bit extra.

Next, there are various cheat options, depending on the numbers with which one is faced.

- Split the big number up: 636 ÷ 12 is the same as (600 ÷ 12) + (36 ÷ 12), which is the same as 50 + 3, which is 53.

- Split the small number into factors: 636 ÷ 12 is the same as 636 ÷ 2 ÷ 6, which is the same as 318 ÷ 6, which is 53.

- Keep dividing all the numbers in half for as long as possible: 636 ÷ 12 is the same as 318 ÷ 6, which is the same as 159 ÷ 3, which is 53.

5. LONG MULTIPLICATION

Say the task at hand is to work out in one's head the number of times one has slept with one's husband during the eight years the two of you have been married—assuming it has averaged out to about once a week for each of the fifty-two weeks of the year, apart from, say, a total of seven weeks off due to being away for work, being too stressed at Christmas, being bitten by a tick in one's nether regions, and so forth.

Thus, the sum that faces one is 45 x 8. Again there are various cheat options:

• Multiply the tens, then the units together: 45 x 8 is the same as (40 x 8) + (5 x 8), which is 360.

• Round up one number to the nearest 10 then adjust at the end: 45 x 8 is the same as (50 x 8) - (5 x 8), which is 360.

• Split it into factors: 45 x 8 is the same as 45 x 2 x 2 x 2, which is 360.

When one is twenty years old, does one ever imagine that one will have sex with the same person 360 times? One does not.

Voting

Tales abound of strange creatures who choose to spend more than a single second of their precious time on earth in a dilemma over whether or not to vote. The more functioning members of the human race appreciate that this is a little like being in a dilemma about whether or not to breathe. Yet there are those who disagree and who regularly fail to make it to the ballot box. Such behavior may be considered perfectly reasonable by some, although one must assume that these people are content to accept the fact that for the next four years or so, they will have *no right whatsoever* to complain about the following: trash collectors, traffic police, bus routes, schools, hospitals, crime, war, or any of the other thousands of issues that our elected representatives attend to. One must also assume that, by abstaining, they are happy to forget those women such as Susan B. Anthony who fought so long and hard for the right to vote. But for those who possess the slightest trace of social/political/moral/ environmental/any conscience, there is simply no excuse not to make the journey to the polling place when required. Alternatively, register to vote by mail, then all you need to do is find the nearest mailbox. For those who are unequal even to this tiny task, there is only one solution: Get thee to Belarus! You do not deserve to live in a stable, democratic society.

DATE WOMEN WON THE RIGHT TO VOTE

Unless otherwise indicated, the date signifies the year women were granted the right both to vote and to run for office.

Year	Country
1788	United States of America (to run for office)
1893	New Zealand (to vote)
1902	Australia*
1906	Finland
1907	Norway (to run for office)*

* Right subject to conditions or restrictions

Year	Country
1913	Norway**
1915	Denmark, Iceland*
1917	Netherlands (to stand for election)
1918	Austria, Canada (to vote),* Estonia, Georgia, Germany, Hungary, Ireland,* Kyrgyzstan, Latvia, Lithuania, Poland, Russian Federation, United Kingdom (restricted to women over thirty)*
1919	Belarus, Belgium (to vote),* Luxembourg, Netherlands (to vote), New Zealand (to run for office), Sweden,* Ukraine
1920	Albania, Canada (to stand for election),* Czechoslovakia, Iceland,** United States of America (to vote)
1921	Armenia, Azerbaijan, Belgium (to run for office),* Sweden**
1924	Kazakhstan, Mongolia, Saint Lucia, Tajikistan
1927	Turkmenistan
1928	Ireland,** United Kingdom (now included all women over twenty-one)**
1929	Ecuador,* Romania*
1930	South Africa ("Whites"), Turkey (to vote)
1931	Chile,* Portugal,* Spain, Sri Lanka
1932	Brazil, Maldives, Thailand, Uruguay
1934	Cuba, Portugal,* Turkey (to run for office)
1937	Philippines
1938	Bolivia,* Uzbekistan
1939	El Salvador (to vote)
1941	Panama*
1942	Dominican Republic
1944	Bulgaria, France, Jamaica
1945	Croatia, Guyana (to run for office), Indonesia, Italy, Japan, Senegal, Slovenia, Togo

** Restrictions or conditions lifted

Year	Country
1946	Cameroon, North Korea, Djibouti (to vote), Guatemala, Liberia, Panama,** Romania,** Trinidad and Tobago, Venezuela, Vietnam, Yugoslavia
1947	Argentina, Malta, Mexico (to vote), Pakistan, Singapore
1948	Belgium,** Israel, Niger, South Korea, Seychelles, Suriname
1949	Chile,** China, Costa Rica, Syria (to vote)*
1950	Barbados, Canada (to vote),** Haiti, India
1951	Antigua and Barbuda, Dominica, Grenada, Nepal, Saint Kitts and Nevis, Saint Vincent and the Grenadines
1952	Bolivia,** Côte d'Ivoire, Greece, Lebanon
1953	Bhutan, Guyana (to vote), Mexico (to run for office), Syria**
1954	Belize, Colombia, Ghana
1955	Cambodia, Eritrea, Ethiopia, Honduras, Nicaragua, Peru
1956	Benin, Comoros, Egypt, Gabon, Mali, Mauritius, Somalia
1957	Malaysia, Zimbabwe (to vote)**
1958	Burkina Faso, Chad, Guinea, Laos, Nigeria (South)
1959	Madagascar, San Marino (to vote), Tunisia, Tanzania
1960	Canada (to run for office),** Cyprus, Gambia, Tonga
1961	Bahamas,* Burundi, El Salvador (to run for office), Malawi, Mauritania, Paraguay, Rwanda, Sierra Leone
1962	Algeria, Australia,** Monaco, Uganda, Zambia
1963	Afghanistan, Republic of the Congo, Equatorial Guinea, Fiji, Iran, Kenya, Morocco, Papua New Guinea (to run for office)

Year	Country
1964	Bahamas,** Libya, Papua New Guinea (to vote), Sudan
1965	Botswana, Lesotho
1967	Democratic Republic of the Congo (to vote), Ecuador,** Kiribati, Tuvalu
1968	Nauru, Swaziland
1970	Andorra (to vote), Republic of the Congo (to run for office)
1971	Switzerland
1972	Bangladesh
1973	Andorra (to run for office), Bahrain, San Marino (to run for office)
1974	Jordan, Solomon Islands
1975	Angola, Cape Verde, Mozambique, São Tomé and Principe, Vanuatu
1976	Portugal**
1977	Guinea-Bissau
1978	Nigeria (North), Zimbabwe (to run for office)
1979	Marshall Islands, Micronesia, Palau
1980	Iraq
1984	Lichtenstein, South Africa ("Coloureds and Indians")
1986	Central African Republic, Djibouti (to run for office)
1989	Namibia
1990	Samoa
1994	South Africa ("Blacks")
2005	Kuwait

Saudia Arabia and Vatican City are currently the only countries where men are allowed to vote and women are not.

Source: Inter-Parliamentary Union (www.ipu.org)

Bras

T-shirt

Balconette

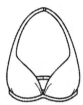

Halter neck

Push-up

Backless

Trainer/triangle

Sports

Nursing

Chicken fillet

No bra

Group Sex

POPULAR COMBINATIONS
FOR GROUP SEX

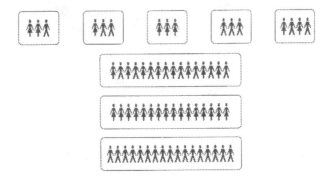

The etiquette of group sex varies considerably according to context. The main pitfalls to watch out for are outlined below.

IN A PRIVATE HOME (SPONTANEOUS)

In this scenario, the trickiest moment tends to occur when the idea of group sex is initially proposed. Whomsoever it falls upon to do this places herself in a highly vulnerable position; hence, regardless of the response of the friends and/or acquaintances present, she is under no circumstances to be made to feel embarrassed or uncomfortable in any way. To be brave and open enough to suggest group sex in the first place is worthy of applause, period. (She may just be drunk, however, or even high. Still.)

If group sex is your sort of thing, then tally-ho. However, if it happens not to be—which simply by the law of averages may well be the case—it is nonetheless important to respond to the suggestion politely and gracefully. Try to view it as akin to receiving an invitation to go night caving or to stroke someone's pet snake—one might not feel it is quite one's cup of tea, but it is always nice to be asked, and for that one should be appreciative. A simple "Gosh, what a lovely offer, but I'm okay, actually" should suffice. (Either way, it is advisable to take a moment to think through in advance what one's reaction would be if the opportunity ever presented itself. This prevents all manner of awkwardness that can arise from indecision.)

If, on the other hand, you find yourself on the receiving end of a rebuff, it is proper to respond equally politely and gracefully—"No problem. But if you ever change your mind . . ." The aim is to imply that the offer remains, yet without anyone feeling pressured. Then swiftly move the evening on—organize another round of drinks, suggest another round of bridge, begin a game of charades . . . whatever. Do not under any circumstances leave the gathering for at least thirty minutes after the suggestion has been made; to leave sooner is to imply that one is embarrassed, an entirely unwarranted sentiment assuming the others present have approached the situation in the proper way.

IN A PRIVATE HOME (PREPLANNED)

There are organizations that arrange for group sex to occur in a preplanned manner. Some of these, such as One Leg Up (www.onelegupnyc.com), are specifically female-friendly. One advantage of this approach is that those involved do not generally know one another—though this can also be a disadvantage, of course.

Either way, this option allows one the opportunity to arrive prepared, and for a game plan to be worked out before diving in. Elements of the game plan might include: know the boundaries; be accompanied by a trusted boyfriend, girlfriend, or friend; bring protection; and so forth.

As with planting a new garden or shopping for Christmas presents, it is when, where, and how to take the initial plunge that tend to be the most daunting elements of the process. Remember that everyone is nervous. Initiate some conversation, but make sure this is kept to the impersonal: the weather, vacation destinations, and recent films seen or books read all work well as topics to steer toward. If at any point you see someone you know from another context—whether from work, from the dry cleaners, or from the pages of a magazine—be discreet. They too have the right to pursue and explore.

The moment will come when it is necessary—desirable, hopefully—to address the matter at hand. There is no getting away from the fact that at this point what one needs is a fair amount of chutzpah, coupled with a stiff drink.

Be assured that many of the usual rules of social interaction continue to apply in a group-sex scenario. Do not monopolize the handsomest man or woman at the party. Be generous with introductions. Make sure everyone feels included. At any point in the proceedings, feel free to approach those who interest or attract you. In Europe, it is acceptable in this context to touch someone in a nonsexual place as a form of nonverbal proposition; in the U.S., however, it is considered impolite to presume to touch someone without asking permission. If, while engaged in sexual activity, one is approached by someone who does not appeal just at that moment, simply raise a hand and say "We're okay, thanks." Do not attempt to explain. Be polite to everyone, whether you find them attractive or not. After all, as a general rule, it is the uglier men who perform the best, simply because they have more to prove. On the other side, a rebuff of this sort is not to be taken personally. Either way, no means no.

And—obviously—*always* use protection.

AT A SEX CLUB

Alternatively, there are so-called sex clubs, which are rather more public affairs. Sadly, these tend to be somewhat seedy in feel, though no doubt it is only a matter of time before this situation improves—it is beginning to in New York City, for example (try Devious Delights, Rendezvous, or Checkmates). Ideally, however, take a trip to Paris. There, sex clubs are a relatively well-accepted leisure activity akin to going to the cinema or strolling in the park. The city boasts nearly fifty such establishments, but some are inevitably more chic than others so it is important to choose carefully. Beginners should try Chris et Manu or L'Abys, two of the most mainstream, and thus the least daunting. Most cater predominantly to couples or single women, and ban single men. Some include (an often surprisingly delicious) dinner in the price of entry.

Whatever the context, the codes of behavior that govern the end of an evening of group sex are relatively similar. If one loses one's coat, one's bra, or indeed any item of clothing, it is more polite to telephone the following day to inquire as to its whereabouts than to interrupt the host or hostess in whatever they are doing then and there. On taking one's leave, there is no need to say goodbye to everyone—only to those with whom one feels one has built up a particular rapport. And, finally, unlike almost every other sort of social gathering, there is no need to write a thank-you letter.

How to Buy a Bathing Suit

Buying a bathing suit is one of the few areas of clothes shopping where it is simply counterproductive to be a stickler for perfection. Accept that never in the history of the universe has there existed a woman who has looked at herself in the fitting-room mirror while wearing a bathing suit and thought, "By golly, you look fabulous!" Ignore the onslaught of images of the likes of Keira Knightley which promote twenty-first century ideals of what constitutes the perfect body. Instead, focus on the following: airbrushing, airbrushing, and airbrushing—the foremost reason a celebrity looks the way she does in any magazine. The only exceptions to this rule are Madonna (who spends three hours a day working at it, and thus deserves it) and Kate Moss (who doesn't, and doesn't).

The aim, therefore, is simply to limit the trauma inflicted by the task at hand.

PREPARATION

Before embarking on the trip, take all necessary steps toward whatever is a standard level of hair removal. If this means none, then fine. But if this means three hours with the lovely and brilliant Brazilian woman in midtown, so be it; otherwise the battle is already all but lost. Next, be broad-minded in the choice of shop. Bathing suits are not like shoes or bags—one does not get what one pays for—so it is worth trying anywhere from Barneys to Bebe.

THE CHANGING ROOM

Once a selection has been made, the wisdom of Erma Bombeck comes into play: "Women shop for a bikini with more care than they do a husband. The rules are the same. Look for something you'll feel comfortable wearing. Allow for room to grow." Try to focus on the one aspect of your body that you like the most, then look for something that somehow draws attention to it—using bright colors, a pattern, a bow, a belt, embroidery, or ruching, perhaps. Ensure that the top half of the bikini sits comfortably, and similarly, that the bottom half is not digging in anywhere. Also note that if the latter does not seem to be providing enough coverage, it is not a different *size* that is required, but a different design entirely. For advice on which style of bathing suit flatters which particular body shape, simply pick up a copy of any women's magazine around June or July.

THE DECISION

It is important to bear in mind when and where the bathing suit is most likely to be making an appearance. For surfing, a string bikini is off-limits. Ditto for kayaking down the Amazon. For lifeguards, a plain-colored one-piece is mandatory. For the synchronized swimming final at the Olympics, a one-piece is also recommended but cosmetic matters should be factored into the equation: a gold or silver one is the ideal choice here. A thong bikini is acceptable on Copacabana Beach in Rio de Janeiro—nowhere else. And, regardless of context, when it comes to bathing suits, prevailing fashion trends are to be ignored entirely. The single exception to this is the one-piece, which is about to enjoy a significant renaissance. There are an increasing number of designs available that are the opposite of dull—with plunging necklines, cutout waists, halter necks and so on. For tallish women, something along these lines is the ideal choice. If all else fails, muddle through with the least ghastly option but distract the onlooker's eye upward and away from the body with a spectacularly elaborate hairstyle. A "Princess Leia" works particularly well for this purpose.

When it comes to actually donning the bathing suit, it is essential to remind oneself as often as possible that no one is looking. To reiterate, *no one* is looking. They are all far too preoccupied worrying about their own appearance—both the women and, increasingly, the men too.

Memorable Film Lines of the 1930s Through the 1970s

"I want to be alone."
—*Grand Hotel* (1932)

"Oh no, it wasn't the airplanes.
It was Beauty killed the Beast."
—*King Kong* (1933)

"Toto, I've a feeling we're not in Kansas anymore."

—*The Wizard of Oz* (1939)

"As God is my witness, I'll never be hungry again."

—*Gone with the Wind* (1939)

"We'll always have Paris."

—*Casablanca* (1942)

"Oh, Jerry, don't let's ask for the moon. We have the stars."

—*Now, Voyager* (1942)

"We're neither of us free to love each other. There's too much in the way. There's still time, if we control ourselves and behave like sensible human beings. There's still time."

—*Brief Encounter* (1945)

"Story of my life. I always get the fuzzy end of the lollipop."

—*Some Like It Hot* (1959)

"That's the way it crumbles . . . cookie-wise."

—*The Apartment* (1960)

"All of you! You all killed him! And my brother, and Riff. Not with bullets, or guns, with hate. Well now I can kill, too, because now I have hate!"

—*West Side Story* (1961)

"Love means never having to say you're sorry."

—*Love Story* (1970)

"Your girl is lovely, Hubbell."

—*The Way We Were* (1973)

The Personality of a Beehive

How does one determine the personality of a beehive? The unenlightened may well consider this to be a preposterous question, but, in fact, the humble beehive is capable of a gamut of emotions. Not only are they most rewarding to explore from a philosophical and scientific point of view, but a sensitivity to the disposition of a beehive may also spare one unnecessary—and possibly painful—entanglements with the hive's occupants in the future.

THE HAPPY HIVE

Contrary to popular belief, a happy hive does not wish to sting passersby, and the ridiculous flailing and shrieking that commonly accompanies a human encounter with bees is entirely unwarranted. A hive is at its happiest when the air is warm and damp, as this is when bees fly the most easily and plants secrete the most nectar. Happy bees will also pursue an interloper (whether human or otherwise) no further than twelve feet from the hive. A hive betrays its contentment with a deep hum.

THE EUPHORIC SWARM

The bee's greatest joy is the moment of "swarming." This is when the bees gorge themselves before setting off en masse with a queen to establish a new colony. This generally takes place at midday on a fine day, and is accompanied by a tremendous amount of noise. While the great boiling mass of bees may look threatening, it is in fact unlikely to attack as it has no home to protect. Should one encounter a swarm, however, the most sensible thing to do is to telephone one's local beekeeping association to arrange for someone to collect the swarm, which is done by literally "pouring" them into a box and taking them to a new home.

THE UNHAPPY HIVE

An unhappy hive expresses its discontent by emitting an agitated, high-pitched whine, and on these occasions it is wise to steer well clear. During particularly stormy weather conditions, the hive is likely to be of a slightly worse disposition, as it appears that bees are upset by the electrical charge in the atmosphere. Rough handling or bumps from the beekeeper may also upset the colony, which may often retain an unhappy memory for up to a week at a time. Should the hive lose its queen, the colony will also fall into disarray and bad temper unless a new queen is found quickly; otherwise, as an absolute last resort, the colony must be put to death by pouring half a pint of gasoline into the top of the hive.

THE GRIEF-STRICKEN HIVE

By the early nineteenth century, the hive had attained something of the status of a family member in many European households. On the occasion of a death in the family, the ceremony of "telling the bees" was enacted in the belief that this would prevent the grief-stricken bees from ceasing to produce honey, leaving the hive, or passing away altogether. Should one be fortunate enough to be in possession of a beehive, and unfortunate enough to lose a family member, one may consider it prudent to perform a similar ritual:

1. A family member or trusted servant raps the hive three times with the key of the household.

2. The hive is informed "Your master is dead," followed by an entreaty not to leave.

3. The hive is dressed in a black crepe bow.

4. The hive is supplied with food from the funeral gathering.

5. After an appropriate interval, the hive is informed of the identity of its new master, ideally by way of a personal introduction.

A similar ceremony, replacing the black crepe with something gayer such as a red cloth, may also be performed on the occasion of a family wedding.

BEE NATIONALITIES

While one does not like to be prejudiced about these things, nationality can play a key part in determining a bee's disposition. Some well-known types of bees include:

- **Italian bee.** The large, plump, and golden queen breeds gentle bees that produce plentiful honey.

- **British black bee.** Making something of a comeback, it is resilient to disease, but is also known for its "sparky" character and a greater tendency to sting.

- **African killer bee.** Extremely plentiful honey producers but, as the name suggests, not a personality to be trifled with.

In Case of a Genuine Emergency

The likelihood of many of the scenarios outlined below actually happening in our lifetime is widely disputed. As a result, the decision to stock the pantry with fifty boxes of crackers and ten cases of bottled water is entirely a matter of disposition. But for those who would rather know than not know . . .

GENERAL INSTRUCTIONS
FOR ANY NATIONAL EMERGENCY

Retreat indoors, and stay there until advised otherwise. Switch on the radio or television and wait to hear further instructions. Keep calm—mass panic can cause more injuries than anything else. Find out where and how to turn off water, gas, and electricity supplies at home; the emergency procedures at the office or at school; how one's nearest and dearest plan to stay in touch; and if any neighbors need help. The more neurotically minded may also want to put together an emergency kit, either to sustain them through a few days holed up at home or to take with them in case of an evacuation. Suggested contents include:

- A first aid kit, including any regular medication
- Some cash and a credit card
- A battery-powered radio with spare batteries
- A flashlight with spare batteries, as well as candles and matches
- A change of clothes
- A blanket

- Non-perishable food and a can opener
- Bottled water
- Dust mask, duct tape, and plastic sheeting

In the event of . . .

A BOMB EXPLOSION

If the explosion occurs outdoors, stay indoors (away from windows or doors) in case there is a second bomb in the area. If the explosion occurs indoors, evacuate by whatever route possible; if trapped, tap on pipes to try to make contact with rescuers. Do not strike matches—there may be a gas leak.

A CHEMICAL ATTACK

Those in the vicinity of a chemical attack suffer from nausea, blurred vision, and/or breathing difficulties. Also keep an eye out for dead animals.

The priority is to find clean air as quickly as possible. Hence, if the attack occurs outside, retreat indoors at once. Close all doors and windows and shut off any air-conditioning in order to halt the flow of air from outside. Then take shelter in an interior room, if possible sealing it with plastic sheeting and duct tape. Remain there until informed that it is safe to leave. If the attack occurs indoors, evacuate by whatever route possible; if trapped, open all windows and await help.

Once clean air has been found, it is essential to seek professional care. All clothing needs to be decontaminated and the body scrubbed thoroughly with soap and water to prevent any chemicals from spreading further.

A RADIOLOGICAL ATTACK (MOST PROBABLY IN THE FORM OF A "DIRTY" BOMB)

This is initially difficult to identify. The bomb itself will be evident from the explosion, but it might be some time before it is identified as radioactive.

The priority is to avoid inhaling radioactive dust. To this end, follow the procedure described above for a chemical attack, but with one addition—cover the nose and mouth at all times. Also bear in mind that within twenty-four hours, the threat posed by this form of attack reduces dramatically. So try to wait it out.

A BIOLOGICAL ATTACK (FOR EXAMPLE, ANTHRAX OR SMALLPOX)

This can only be identified once other people start to show symptoms. These tend to appear flulike at first, but within a few days become less recognizable—sufferers of smallpox, for instance, will develop a rash of flat, red spots which then turn into blisters. If symptomatic, go to a hospital. If not, minimize all contact with others.

A NUCLEAR ATTACK

This can be identified as such by a huge explosion, a blindingly bright flash of light, intense heat, and a mushroom cloud.

The priority is to avoid the radioactive fallout. To this end, if in the immediate vicinity of the blast it is essential to get out of the path of the radioactive cloud as quickly as possible. Ten minutes' brisk walk should do it, but it is crucial to travel in the correct direction. Aim to move away from the center of the blast, which is wherever the initial bright flash was seen or, failing that, where the most damage to buildings was done. Once this has been located, look up into the sky to see which direction the radioactive cloud is moving—in other words, which way it is being blown by the wind—then head off perpendicular to this. Keep going until out from underneath the cloud (which will not be as far as one might think, probably only a mile or so), then take shelter immediately to avoid being subjected to any residual radiation, as well as to continue to be protected should the wind cause the radioactive cloud to change direction.

If not in the immediate vicinity of the blast, seek shelter underground—in a basement, perhaps. It is imperative to protect oneself from the fallout with as much solid, dense material—such as concrete or earth—as possible. Even piles of books or newspapers will help. If there is nowhere underground to go, any building that is more than ten stories high will also do, but remain at least three stories from the top to avoid any radioactive material that falls on the roof. Stay there for at least forty-eight hours or until instructed that it is safe to leave (radioactive material decays quickly—up to 99% after two days). If possible, decontaminate.

At all times, keep the nose and mouth covered.

AN ASTEROID HITTING THE EARTH

Assuming there is some advance warning, which for an asteroid of any significant size there will be, the priority is to evacuate the area at risk. Otherwise, there is nothing personally one can do—except pray, possibly.

ALIENS LANDING

Be friendly. One never knows what they might have to offer.

Chocolate

THE PROVENANCE OF THE WORLD'S
COCOA BEAN SUPPLY

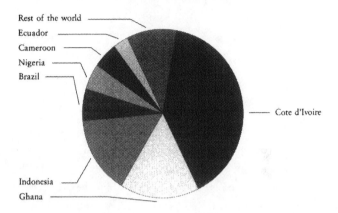

Rest of the world

Ecuador

Cameroon

Nigeria

Brazil

Cote d'Ivoire

Indonesia

Ghana

The three foremost varieties of cocoa beans used in chocolate are criollo, trinitario, and forastero. Of these, criollo is the rarest and most expensive cocoa on the market. A woman who professes not to like any of these—in other words, not to like chocolate—is generally deemed a freak, a liar, or a man in drag. There is still some debate about whether chocolate really is preferable to sex. For those who believe it is, see page 32. Nonetheless, there is no doubt that it is a truly marvelous creation.

The origin of the word *chocolate* is an amalgamation of the Aztec words *xocolli*, meaning "bitter," and *atl*, meaning "water." Cocoa beans, from which chocolate derives, were initially imbibed in the form of a bitter drink, often with copious amounts of chili added. This is not recommended. Christopher Columbus stumbled across cocoa beans in 1502 as he robbed a Mayan trading canoe that was carrying beans as cargo. Columbus initially believed them to be a type of almond: "They seemed to hold these almonds at a great price; for when they were brought on board ship together with their goods, I observed that when any of these almonds fell, they all stooped to pick it up, as if an eye had fallen." In fact, cocoa beans were once a common form of currency in South America.

The melting point of chocolate ranges from 63°F to 97°F, which is slightly below human body temperature which is about 98°F. It is for this reason that it literally melts in your mouth. Americans eat an average of 6 pounds of chocolate per person per year, up from 3.4 pounds in 1980.

Finally, if one learns just one way to make chocolate cake—and after all, why learn more?—use the recipe in Nigella Lawson's *Nigella Bites* (2001). Do not be daunted by the number of ingredients: the preparation technique is miraculously simple, and this is one recipe that turns out just dandy every single time.

The Terminology of Sleeves

Angel sleeve. A long, wide sleeve that flows loosely from the shoulder. The height of fashion in the fourteenth century.

Armlet. A small, short sleeve shaped like a band around the arm.

Bag sleeve. 1. A sleeve that is full to the elbow, tapering at the wrist, and gathered into a wide cuff. Popular in the early fifteenth century. 2. A sleeve that is narrow to the elbow, then bags from the elbow to the wrist. Also fifteenth century.

Balloon sleeve. An extremely full, rounded sleeve, usually lined with buckram or some such fabric, that goes from shoulder to elbow (or sometimes shoulder to wrist). Also known as a *melon sleeve*. A fad in the 1890s.

Barrel sleeve. A barrel-shaped sleeve that tapers from the elbow, where it is at its widest, down to a narrow wrist and up to a natural shoulder. Sometimes with a horizontal seam in the middle.

Batwing sleeve. See **dolman sleeve**.

Bell sleeve. A full sleeve that flares a little at the lower edge like a bell.

Bernhardt sleeve. A long, fitted sleeve, usually with a point over the top of the wrist, with the fabric gathered into the lining in a *mousquetaire* fashion.

Bishop sleeve. A long sleeve that is full in the lower part below the elbow like an Anglican bishop's robe, and either loose or held by a band at the wrist. At the peak of its popularity around 1900.

Bracelet sleeve. A sleeve that reaches below the elbow, about halfway to the wrist—convenient for wearing bracelets, in other words.

Cape sleeve. A loose, full sleeve that hangs freely at the front and the back of the shoulder, like a cape.

Cap sleeve. A short sleeve that just covers the shoulder, but does not continue underneath the arm.

Cornet sleeve. A trumpet-shaped sleeve that ends in a low, bell-like flare.

Cowl sleeve. A sleeve with a cowl drape at the shoulder.

Cubital. A sleeve that only covers the arm from the wrist to the elbow. From the Latin word *cubitum*, meaning "elbow."

Dolman sleeve. A sleeve cut as an extension of the bodice of a dress, shirt, or jacket, designed without a socket for the shoulder. It thus creates a deep, wide armhole that reaches from the waist to a narrowed wrist. Very fashionable in the 1920s, 1930s, and 1980s, then again in the 2000s, by which time it had also become known as a **batwing sleeve.**

Double sleeve. A wide, sometimes flared oversleeve on top of a fitted undersleeve, often in a contrasting color.

Draped elbow sleeve. A straight sleeve that reaches to the elbow, where it ends in a draped, loose fold to suggest a wide sleeve that has been turned back. Common in the seventeenth and eighteenth centuries.

Elbow sleeve. A sleeve that extends to or slightly beyond the elbow.

Envelope sleeve. A sleeve that is full at the shoulder, pleated in triangular folds.

Foresleeve. 1. A section of a sleeve that covers the forearm. 2. An extra, decorative sleeve. Often removable.

Free Action sleeve. A trade term for a type of sleeve that has an additional section under the arm that allows increased freedom of movement.

Funnel sleeve. A sleeve shaped like a funnel, funnily enough, with the top turned back to form a cuff. An invention of the sixteenth century.

Gigot. See **leg-of-mutton sleeve.**

Goddess sleeve. A sleeve that billows out gracefully below the elbow, then is gathered in again twice before reaching the wrist. For the best examples of goddess fashion generally, refer to the near-perfect film *One Touch of Venus* (1948) starring Ava Gardner and Robert Walker.

Half sleeve. 1. A removable mini-sleeve that covers only the forearm. Usually made of lace or sheer fabric. Worn for extra warmth. 2. A sleeve protector worn by clerical workers.

Hanging sleeve. A coat sleeve that hangs down at the side, but with a slit in the front for the arm itself to peep through. The arm was often then covered with an elaborately decorated shirt or blouse sleeve. Most popular in the fifteenth century.

Kimono sleeve. An extra large sleeve panel set into a deep armhole that extends from the shoulder to the waist.

Lapped sleeve. A short sleeve with the fabric lapped backward or forward at the shoulder to give the effect of a fold.

Leg-of-mutton sleeve. A sleeve shaped like a leg of mutton. It fits tightly from the wrist to the elbow, then balloons out from the elbow to the shoulder, where it is gathered or pleated into the bodice of the garment. Most fashionable in the Edwardian period, then again during the Edwardian revival period of the late 1960s and early 1970s. Also called a **gigot**.

Mancheron. Worn by women in the mid-sixteenth century, a mancheron is a sleeve that is attached to the top of the shoulder and hangs loosely down the back of the arm.

Melon sleeve. See **balloon sleeve.**

Mousquetaire sleeve. A long, fitted sleeve that for decorative purposes is shirred (i.e., gathered into two or more parallel rows) lengthwise from shoulder to wrist and softly draped.

Oversleeve. A sleeve worn over another sleeve known as an **undersleeve**, sometimes held together by a collar piece. Often made of fur.

Pagoda sleeve. A three-quarter-length or half-length sleeve style that is frilled to the elbow where it then widens into either several tiers of flounces or one large flounce seamed to curve in a shape that somewhat resembles a pagoda. The flounces are often decorated with bows or ribbons. Widely seen among upper-class women in the nineteenth century.

Peasant sleeve. A long, full sleeve set into a dropped shoulder and gathered into a band at the wrist.

Puff sleeve. A short sleeve that is gathered into the shoulder segment of a garment to create a puffed effect. An eminently elegant creation.

Push-up sleeve. A three-quarter-length or full-length sleeve with the fullness shirred to a band, with the result that when it is pushed up the arm it becomes a shorter, puffed sleeve.

Raglan sleeve. A sleeve designed to allow the arms greater mobility, it extends from the neckline to the wrist, joined to the bodice by diagonal seams from the neck to under the arms. Named after Lord Raglan (1788–1855), British Commander during the Crimean War.

Shoulder-puff sleeve. A long sleeve with a bit of a puff at the shoulder, but fitted from there to the wrist. The predecessor of a sleeve with many puffs all along its length that was popular under the Tudors.

Virago sleeve. An excessively full sleeve tied at intervals to form puffs. Common in the seventeenth century.

How to Clean a Pearl Necklace

Pearls were once so expensive that the Roman general Vitellius is said to have financed an entire military campaign by selling just one of his mother's pearl earrings. Historically, pearls were found naturally in oyster beds in the Persian Gulf, the Red Sea, and along the coasts of India and Sri Lanka, but today most tend to be cultured—encouraged into existence by humans, in other words.

Pearls should be cleaned every time they are worn. Merely by coming into contact with the skin, they absorb the acid contained within it, which over time can be very harmful to the surface appearance of the pearls. Similarly, makeup, perfume, and hair spray all cause them to deteriorate in quality. Never use a commercial jewelry cleaner—these almost always contain undesirable amounts of ammonia. Instead, simply wipe each individual pearl with a slightly damp cloth. About every fifth time they are worn, a more thorough cleaning is recommended. Use a soft cloth dipped in mild soapy water (never dishwashing liquid), then remove any soap residue with a different damp cloth, and leave the necklace to dry. Store it in a silk, satin, or velvet pouch (never a plastic one, which will cause the pearls to dry out and crack).

Pets

The three most popular names for pets are Max, Sam, and Lady. But to what kind of domestic companion should one ascribe this endearing moniker? Let the pets of the famous provide a guide (or warning) of sorts.

PERSON	PET	PET'S NAME
Odysseus (sometime around 1200–1300 B.C.)	Dog	Argos

ADDITIONAL INFORMATION

Probably the first dog ever written about. The relevant passage[1] in Homer's *The Odyssey* has made many a grown-up weep, especially when read in the Robert Fitzgerald verse translation (1961).

---

1 An extract from book 17 of Homer's *The Odyssey* where Odysseus, disguised as a beggar, finally reaches his palace in Ithaka:

> While he spoke
> an old hound, lying near, pricked up his ears
> and lifted up his muzzle. This was Argos,
> trained as a puppy by Odysseus,
> but never taken on a hunt before
> his master sailed for Troy. The young men, afterward,
> hunted wild goats with him, and hare, and deer,
> but he had grown old in his master's absence.
> Treated as rubbish now, he lay at last
> upon a mass of dung before the gates—
> manure of mules and cows, piled there until
> fieldhands could spread it on the king's estate.
> Abandoned there, and half destroyed by flies,
> old Argos lay.
>
> But when he knew he heard
> Odysseus' voice nearby, he did his best
> to wag his tail, nose down, with flattened ears,
> having no strength to move nearer his master.
> And the man looked away,
> wiping a salt tear from his cheek; but he
> hid this from Eumaios. Then he said:
>
> 'I marvel that they leave this hound to lie
> here on the dung pile;
> he would have been a fine dog, from the look of him,
> though I can't say as to his power and speed
> when he was young. You find the same good build
> in house dogs, table dogs landowners keep
> all for style.'

PERSON	PET	PET'S NAME
Isaac Newton (1643–1727)	Cat	Spitface

ADDITIONAL INFORMATION

For whom Newton invented the first-ever kitty door.

PERSON	PET	PET'S NAME
Lord Byron (1788–1824)	Dog (Newfoundland)	Boatswain

ADDITIONAL INFORMATION

Byron wrote a poem about him when he died.[2]

> *And you replied, Eumaios:*
>
> *'A hunter owned him—but the man is dead*
> *in some far place. If this old hound could show*
> *the form he had when Lord Odysseus left him,*
> *going to Troy, you'd see him swift and strong.*
> *He never shrank from any savage thing*
> *he'd brought to bay in the deep woods; on the scent*
> *no other dog kept up with him. Now misery*
> *has him in leash. His owner died abroad,*
> *and here the women slaves will take no care of him.*
> *You know how servants are: without a master*
> *they have no will to labour, or excel.*
> *For Zeus who views the wide world takes away*
> *half the manhood of a man, that day*
> *he goes into captivity and slavery.'*
>
> *Eumaios crossed the court and went straight forward*
> *into the megaron among the suitors;*
> *but death and darkness in that instant closed*
> *the eyes of Argos, who had seen his master,*
> *Odysseus, after twenty years.*

2   "Epitaph to a Dog" by Lord Byron:

> *Near this Spot*
> *are deposited the Remains of one*
> *who possessed Beauty without Vanity,*
> *Strength without Insolence,*
> *Courage without Ferosity,*
> *and all the Virtues of Man without his Vices.*
> *This praise, which would be unmeaning Flattery*
> *if inscribed over human Ashes,*
> *is but a just tribute to the Memory of*
> *BOATSWAIN, a DOG,*
> *who was born at Newfoundland, May, 1803,*
> *and died at Newstead, Nov 18th, 1808.*

55

PERSON	PET	PET'S NAME
Elizabeth Barrett Browning (1806–1861)	Dog (Cavalier King Charles Spaniel)	Flush

ADDITIONAL INFORMATION

Kidnapped a total of three times, a common occurrence at the time for London dogs of the genteel classes. Her owner wrote a poem about her.[3] Also one of the few dogs to boast her own biography: *Flush* by Virginia Woolf, written as a sort of memorial to Woolf's own spaniel Pinka.

PERSON	PET	PET'S NAME
Charles Dickens (1812–1870)	Cat	Willamena

ADDITIONAL INFORMATION

Willamena kept Dickens company in his study as he wrote, and when she wanted his attention she would snuff out his reading candle.

PERSON	PET	PET'S NAME
Florence Nightingale (1820–1910)	Owl	Athena

ADDITIONAL INFORMATION

A fierce, expressive bird, Athena traveled in Nightingale's pocket and learned how to bow and curtsey.

---

3   Extract from "To Flush, My Dog" by Elizabeth Barrett Browning:

> *Loving friend, the gift of one*
> *Who her own true faith has run*
> *Through thy lower nature,*
> *Be my benediction said*
> *With my hand upon thy head,*
> *Gentle fellow-creature!*
> *Like a lady's ringlets brown,*
> *Flow thy silken ears adown*
> *Either side demurely*
> *Of thy silver-suited breast*
> *Shining out from all the rest*
> *Of thy body purely.*

PERSON	PET	PET'S NAME
Leonard Woolf (1880–1969)	Marmoset	Mitz

ADDITIONAL INFORMATION

Acquired in 1934, Mitz accompanied Leonard everywhere for a time, perching on his shoulder or inside his waistcoat. He even helped protect Woolf, who was Jewish, while on a visit to Germany with his wife Virginia in 1935.[4]

PERSON	PET	PET'S NAME
Paris Hilton (1981–)	Dog (Chihuahua)	Tinkerbell

ADDITIONAL INFORMATION

Born on Halloween 2002 in Athens, Greece.

Statistically, it is dogs who inspire the most great (and not-so-great) literature—marmosets and owls, not so much. These days, the choice of pets is wider than ever, sometimes overwhelmingly so. Increasingly fashionable are tortoises. To track one down, contact American Tortoise Rescue (www.tortoise.com / 1-800-938-3553) which rehouses unwanted tortoises. Alternatively, for a really low-maintenance pet, contact the Butterfly & Nature Gift Store (http://www.butterfly-gifts.com / 1-800-485-1497). They supply caterpillars, which can be observed in their hatching house as they develop into butterflies, at which point they are set free. They only last three to five weeks, so they are perfect for those with a low boredom threshold.

---

4 From *Downhill All the Way* by Leonard Woolf (1967):

> *". . . for mile after mile the crowd shouted 'Heil Hitler!, Heil Hitler!' to Mitz and gave her (and secondarily Virginia and me) the Hitler salute with the outstretched arm . . . It was obvious to the most anti-Semitic stormtrooper that no one who had on his shoulder such a 'dear little thing' could be a Jew."*

Drink Myths

There is a lot of guff talked about alcohol. The topic can turn perfectly intelligent individuals into credulous sots who are willing to believe anything. Invariably, in conversations about drink, fallacious scientific theories and superstitious balderdash go bizarrely unquestioned. It is always worth remembering that it is usually the person (generally, it must be said, a man) holding forth the loudest on the quality of the wine, or malt whiskey, or whatever the drink may be, who is also spouting the most nonsense. Here are some common myths that should politely but firmly be put to rest:

PUTTING WATER IN YOUR WHISKEY IS SACRILEGE

In fact, any distiller will tell you that adding water to whiskey (up to around 1/3 water to 2/3 whiskey) is an excellent way of bringing out the flavors and aromas, and anyone who sneers at this practice is quite wrong to do so. Adding ice, however, will close down the whiskey's flavor, and is a serve best reserved for the times when one would rather not taste the spirit in question.

BITS OF CORK IN THE WINE MEAN IT IS CORKED

While it is undoubtedly tiresome if there are bits of cork in one's wine, it does not necessarily mean the wine is corked. The term "corked" does not in fact refer to the cork itself but to a substance known as TCA that is sometimes produced when chlorine solutions used to sterilize corks come into contact with mold in the cork. A wine that *is* corked will smell akin to a damp towel that has been at the bottom of the laundry basket for three weeks.

A wine may also suffer from being oxidized, in which case it would smell stale, or from sulphur taint, which would cause it to smell of rotten eggs or a struck match.

WINES WITH SCREWCAPS,
RATHER THAN CORKS, ARE LOW QUALITY

Screwcaps help prevent wine from becoming corked. As a result, a growing number of top-end winemakers now use screwcaps, *particularly* for their best wines.

GIN MAKES YOU SAD

In fact, compared to most other spirits, gin is exceptionally low in "congeners"—one of the main causes of hangovers—and is therefore far less likely to leave one sad and headachy in the morning.

A SILVER SPOON IN THE TOP OF THE BOTTLE
KEEPS THE FIZZ IN CHAMPAGNE

This flies utterly in the face of all the laws of physics. The only way to slow down the loss of sparkle is either to stick a stopper in the top or to keep the bottle in the fridge, which slows the release of carbon dioxide.

OLDER WINE IS BETTER THAN YOUNGER WINE

It depends entirely on the type of wine.

BEER GIVES ONE A BEER BELLY,
WHILE SPIRITS DO NOT

Recent research suggests that a propensity for a beer belly is to be blamed on one's genes (in addition, possibly, to a weakening of resolve when in a pizza joint at the end of an evening's imbibing).

RED WINE FOR RED MEAT,
WHITE WINE FOR FISH

Not necessarily. A light, dry red may go perfectly with a fish dish when a full-bodied, sweeter white would not. Consider the wine in the same way one would consider seasoning a dish—a grind of pepper, for example, may enhance both a steak and a bowl of strawberries. Above all, however, one must drink what one jolly well likes.

Cardiopulmonary Resuscitation

In 1767, the Dutch Humane Society issued the following guidelines for performing resuscitation: "Keep the victim warm, give mouth-to-mouth ventilation, and perform insufflation of smoke of burning tobacco into the rectum." Alternative approaches prior to the twentieth century have included the victim being flogged, stuffed into a barrel and rolled down a hill, tied to a trotting horse, covered with hot ashes, and prayed for. Times have moved on, however, and now external chest compressions are generally thought to be the best option in situations of modern cardiopulmonary resuscitation, or CPR.

First, double check that there really are no signs of breathing or a pulse. If there are not, ensure that the patient's airway is clear of vomit or other obstructions. Pinch the patient's nose, tilt the head back to open the airway, then cover his or her mouth with yours and blow out two long, slow breaths, one right after the other.

If there is no reaction, follow this with chest compressions. With the heels of the hands placed on top of one another in a palm-to-back fashion and the fingers interlaced, find a spot directly in between the nipples in the middle of the chest just above the lower tip of the breastbone, and use the heels of the hands to push down an inch or two relatively forcefully, afterward lifting your hands back enough to allow the chest to recoil slightly. Repeat this thirty times (it used to be fifteen but guidelines have recently changed) at a rate of a little faster than one a second, or about 100 a minute. Ensure that you are leaning forward a little so that your shoulders are over your hands; this will allow you to use the weight of your upper body to increase your strength, rather than tiring out your arms.

Repeat five times this cycle of two breaths to every thirty chest compressions, then check again for signs of breathing or a pulse. Continue this cycle until an effect is seen or help arrives. (This may take some time.)

Then ask someone to make you a strong cup of coffee.

Martinis

In recent times, the term "martini" has come to mean anything strong, cold, and in a Y-shaped glass. Yet a truly authentic martini should only ever be made from top-quality gin and/or vodka, with a little vermouth and possibly a dash of bitters.

Any aspirant martini-maker should take care to store her gin and vodka in the freezer at all times. To shake or to stir one's martini remains a moot point. Some experts argue that shaking with ice "bruises" the gin, and alters the flavor for the worse—if this is true, it does so on a scale undetectable to most human palates.

What is certain, however, is that shaking does drive tiny air bubbles, and shards of ice, into the cocktail, making it slightly more dilute than one that is merely stirred with ice. In short, it is simply a matter of personal taste. Either way, the cocktail must be strained into a chilled glass—preferably straight from the freezer.

The art of the martini lies in making infinitesimal changes with dramatic effect. Some variations on the classic recipe include:

- **Traditional dry martini**: 2 1/2 shots of gin or vodka and 3/4 of a shot of extra dry vermouth, stirred with ice and the addition of a dash of orange bitters, served with olive or lemon twist

- **Bradford martini**: a Traditional, shaken rather than stirred

- **Franklin martini**: served with two olives, no bitters

- **Dirty martini**: served with a splash of olive brine and an olive, no bitters

- **Gibson martini**: served with two cocktail onions, no bitters

- **Wet martini**: heavy on the vermouth

- **Vesper martini**: 3 shots of gin, 1 shot of vodka, and 1/2 a shot of vermouth, served with a lemon twist, no bitters.

The truly sophisticated cocktail drinker confines herself to one of the above. The less ascetic palate may require the addition of fruit or liqueurs (and often the subtraction of vermouth), and many modern martini recipes now pander to these tastes. There are as many martini recipes as there are bartenders, but some of the more common ones include:

- **Apple martini**: vodka, apple juice, and either apple schnapps or simple syrup (sugar syrup, which can be bought or made at home by dissolving 2 cups of sugar in 1 cup boiling water, reducing, and then allowing to cool). *Approachable but somewhat dull.*

- **Espresso martini**: vodka, cold espresso, Kahlua coffee liqueur, and simple syrup. *The alcoholic equivalent of class A drugs.*

- **English martini**: rosemary muddled in the bottom of a shaker, then stirred with gin, elderflower cordial, and simple syrup. *Ladylike, and yet a suitably unusual choice.*

- **Chocolate martini**: vodka, crème de cacao, and extra dry vermouth. *To be consumed only in the company of friends.*

- **Lychee martini**: vodka, lychee liqueur, and lychee syrup. *Delicate and fragrant, possibly now a little 1990s.*

- **Lemon martini**: lemon vodka, lemon juice, simple syrup, cointreau, and orange bitters. *Stands or falls entirely on the quality of the lemon vodka.*

- **Martinez**: gin, sweet vermouth, cointreau, simple syrup, and orange bitters. *Supposed to be the forerunner of the martini, and excellent for creating an air of knowledgeability when ordering.*

The Blues

Got the blues? At least have them in an unusual fashion— the Bremen blues, the Olympic blues, or the Pompeian blues, perhaps. These colors have always existed, but it is only in recent years that paint manufacturers and computer programmers have bothered to invent a name for them. Let the lengthy list below shame you into allowing some color other than black an outing to the office tomorrow.[1]

academy blue	Bordeaux blue
Adam blue	Botticelli blue
air blue	Bremen blue
Airforce blue	Brunswick blue
Alice blue	cadet blue
amethyst	Cambridge blue
Antwerp blue	campanula
aqua	canard
azuline	celestine
azure	cerulean
azurine	chambray
baby blue	Charron blue
Berlin blue	chasseur blue
bice	China blue
bloom	ching
blue violet	chinoline blue
bluebell	chow
bluebird	ciel
bluet	clair de lune
blunket	clematis
bonny blue	Cleopatra

---

1 An alternative approach is simply to rebel, in the time-honored tradition, against the rejection of black as one's color of choice, this time employing as justification the manner in which Democritus (ca. 460– ca. 370 B.C.) viewed such frivolities: "By convention there is color, by convention sweetness, by convention bitterness, but in reality there are atoms and space." (With atoms as we know them not yet discovered in the fourth century B.C., in this context the word refers to a concept, coinvented by Democritus, which states that all matter is made up of a number of indivisible, imperishable elements.)

cobalt blue

cobalt turquoise

Copenhagen blue

cornflower blue

coventry blue

cyan

dark blue

dark cyan

dark slate blue

dark turquoise

deep sky blue

Delft blue

delphinium blue

Devonshire blue

Dodger blue

Dresden blue

duck-egg blue

empire blue

ensign

Eton blue

Flemish blue

forget-me-not blue

French blue

French navy

French ultramarine

garter blue

gentian

German blue

gobelin blue

grotto

grulla

heather

horizon blue

hyacinth blue

ice blue

imperial blue

Indanthrone blue

indigo

ink

International Klein blue

iris

Japan blue

Jersey blue

jockey club

kingfisher blue

King's blue

Labrador blue

lapidary blue

lapis lazuli

larkspur

lead blue

light blue

light sky blue

light steel blue

lime blue

Littler's blue

mackerel blue

madonna blue

mallard blue

manganese blue

marine blue

matelot blue

Maya blue

mazarine blue

medium aquamarine

medium blue

medium slate blue

midnight blue

Milori blue

mineral blue

mist

molybdenum blue

moros

National blue

Nattier blue

navy

nile blue

nippon

Olympic blue

Oxford blue

pansy

Paris blue

patent blue

pavonazzo

peacock blue

periwinkle

Persian blue

pervenche blue

petrol blue

plunket

poilu blue

Pompeian blue

powder blue

Prussian blue

Reckitt's blue

robin's egg blue

royal blue

Russian blue

Sanders blue

sapphire

saxe blue

Scotch blue

Sèvres blue

sky blue

slate blue

smalt

steel blue

stone blue

telegraph blue

Thalo blue

Thénard's blue

turkin

Turnbull's blue

turquoise

twilight blue

Tyrian blue

ultramarine

venet

Venetian blue

vessey

Vienna blue

watchet

Wedgwood blue

woad

Yale blue

zenith blue

Zircon blue

Low Spirits

To: Lady Georgiana Morpeth
Foston, Feb. 16th, 1820

Dear Lady Georgiana,

Nobody has suffered more from low spirits than I have done—so I feel for you. 1st. Live as well as you dare. 2nd. Go into the shower—bath with a small quantity of water at a temperature low enough to give you a slight sensation of cold, 75 or 80°. 3rd. Amusing books. 4th. Short views of human life—not further than dinner or tea. 5th. Be as busy as you can. 6th. See as much as you can of those friends who respect and like you. 7th. And of those acquaintances who amuse you. 8th. Make no secret of low spirits to your friends, but talk of them freely—they are always worse for dignified concealment. 9th. Attend to the effects tea and coffee produce upon you. 10th. Compare your lot with that of other people. 11th. Don't expect too much from human life—a sorry business at the best. 12th. Avoid poetry, dramatic representations (except comedy), music, serious novels, melancholy sentimental people, and everything likely to excite feeling or emotion not ending in active benevolence. 13th. Do good, and endeavour to please everybody of every degree. 14th. Be as much as you can in the open air without fatigue. 15th. Make the room where you commonly sit, gay and pleasant. 16th. Struggle by little and little against idleness. 17th. Don't be too severe upon yourself or underrate yourself but do yourself justice. 18th. Keep good blazing fires. 19th. Be firm and constant in the exercise of rational religion. 20th. Believe me, dear Lady Georgiana.

Your devoted servant,
Sydney Smith

Cars

. . . are destroying the planet.

But for those who really must have one—for whom car-sharing or public transport are genuinely not viable options—then, pray, choose carefully. Buying a car is not just about how much money you can afford to spend: your car reveals more about you to other people than perhaps any other purchase you make, apart from shoes (and for men, wristwatches). Hence, deciding factors include not just the dull ones such as "what color?" or "new or secondhand?"[1] (although these are important); far more crucial is, "what sort of car best matches *me*?"

For the unimaginative, there are a plethora of creepily friendly Ford, Saturn, and Toyota dealerships that will offer you a delightful car with good fuel economy, metallic paint, a CD player, air conditioning, and go-faster stripes. If you absolutely insist on going down this route (if you need a practical, reliable everyday car for your family), then a vast array of monthly car magazines exist to help you with the decision. An SUV of any kind is never, ever acceptable: it screams, "Hello, idiot approaching" louder than pretty much any other consumer decision you will ever make in your life. Mystifyingly, Kate Moss drives a Range Rover. Granted, for those who feel absolutely compelled to own an SUV, a Range Rover is the only brand that is even approaching the acceptable, but still. Boo hiss.

If you feel more adventurous (and you should), then looking further afield tends to prove infinitely

---

1   To which the answer is *always* secondhand. The moment you drive your "new" car out of the dealership you are effectively losing 30% of its value in an instant. And that can be a very expensive instant if you're driving out of a Mercedes, BMW, or Bentley dealership.

more rewarding. The dreamers among us are often the first to consider "classic" cars. These always look spectacular, but remember these cars are classics precisely because they were built *a long time ago*. So forget extras like power steering, a decent stereo, or climate control which would have seemed like impossible luxuries to the men (and they were men, not robotic arms) who built these cars. Furthermore, they tend not to be that reliable. It is never wise to rely on a classic car if you ever have to be somewhere at a certain time—for example, if you have a job.

If you are happy to forego the Citroen DS, the Sunbeam Alpine, the MGB, the BMW 2002, the Triumph Herald, the TR7, and others (all decent enough in their own right but surely weekend cars and nothing more), then it is preferable to seek out a car that is of a more modern vintage, yet manages to retain some sense of "character." European cars often seem to have this particular feature factory-fitted. One example is the Jaguar XJ6. Redesigned in the 1990s with a "retro" feel, this car is luxurious (acres of wood and leather), well-equipped (for the time), and yet will probably cost you less than a new Daihatsu Charade. They are great cars and often well looked after by their golf-clubbing, gin-and-tonic-drinking former owners. For those under six feet with an eye for glamour, the Jaguar XJS is also worth considering—particularly the later 1994–1996 models with the straight-6 engine.

For Jaguar, also read BMW and Mercedes. Both of these European carmakers produce motor vehicles that last a very long time, yet whose high-end models have a similar rate of depreciation that is well worth taking advantage of: The Mercedes 500s of the late 1980s, the BMW 7 Series (an early 1990s model—technically sophisticated, mechanically sound) and the Mercedes E series of the mid-1990s are all excellent options.

Another make of car with character is the Saab. Saab was a fully Swedish company (and somewhat eccentric—they also build jet fighters) until the late 1990s when General Motors bought it and homogenized most of the styling right out of the design; but certainly the 900 series of the late 1980s and early 1990s is worth looking at, and not terribly expensive (even the convertibles). The Volvos of the early 1990s—the 240DL and the estate version of the same car—are also cars that will run for a very long time, are easy and cheap to maintain, and are available for not much money (despite now being filmmakers' shorthand for "these characters are cool"—Jarvis Cocker of the band Pulp famously drove a 240DL Estate).

The new Mini (Madonna's vehicle of choice) should also be considered. While annoying the Mini purists with its distinctively "non-Mini" measurements (when put side by side with most hatchbacks, the new Mini is pretty much the same size), the car does have the advantage of a unique retro look combined with contemporary BMW engineering, which means it must be recommended—albeit only in one of the better color schemes such as the gold, the silvery blue, or the cream.

Bear in mind that with many of the cars with larger engines, there is also the option of converting them to run them on biofuels (such as vegetable oil, the drawback to this being that the vehicle then smells like a fryer all the time) or LPG (liquid petroleum gas)—in which case you have the huge advantage of combining a good-looking car with the fact that that you are destroying the planet at a marginally lower rate than at least most of the other drivers in front of you on the freeway.

However, if a car with character is less important to you than your children living longer than thirty-five years when the planet finally disappears under the rising waters of the oceans, a hybrid is the way to go. Sadly, none of the hybrid models currently available are particularly stylish or interesting (except for possibly the new much-lauded Californian "sports" electric car, the Tesla Roadster, which is pretty enough, but awfully expensive), but there is no doubt that the number of MPGs (miles per gallon) they are able to achieve does put petrol cars to shame. The Toyota Prius is popular among celebrities and available in several "styles"—hatchback or saloon—both hideous. Honda makes the Civic and Accord hybrids, along with the Insight. Lexus also offers an SUV hybrid and a luxury-class hybrid. All these cars are worth seriously considering for their environmentally beneficial impact; but, with most of the car industry now aware of the commercial success and mass appeal of hybrids, one can only hope that the next few years will bring hybrid cars with a bit more personality to match.

The alternative, of course, is simply to walk. The colorful and mysterious Edwardian playboy Harry Bensley dedicated seven years of his life to trying to walk all the way around the world with nothing but an iron mask and a pram full of postcards to assist him.[2] Who needs a car anyway?

---

2 The tale goes like this. One summer night in 1907, Harry Bensley was enjoying a raucous dinner at the Sporting Club in London with the fifth Earl of Lonsdale and J. P. Morgan, the most famous financier in the world. As the alcohol flowed and the room grew hazy with cigar smoke, a heated discussion erupted between this motley crew of moneymakers over whether, in a world of ever-shrinking frontiers, it would be possible to walk all the way around the globe without anyone finding out the walker's identity. In the heat of the moment, Morgan bet $100,000 (£21,000) on the fact that it wasn't. It was the largest sum of money ever gambled. Much to Morgan's surprise, and even chagrin, Harry accepted the challenge. It was to change his life forever.

Morgan attached strict and sometimes bizarre conditions to the bet. Harry had to pass through 169 towns around Britain, all in a set order, after which he was to embark upon a tour of 125 towns in eighteen countries all over the world, including Australia, Canada, Persia, Italy, Japan, Egypt, China, and India. The trip was to be financed solely from the proceeds of postcards he sold en route. The postcards were to be stored in a pram that he had to push every step of the way. In an additional twist, he somehow had to find himself a wife. And there was one last, crucial element to the expedition. To obscure his identity, Harry had to wear an iron mask—at all times. To this end, Morgan paid for a minder to accompany Harry to ensure that none of the conditions of the bet were broken. On January 1, 1908, cheering crowds gathered in Trafalgar Square to wave Harry off on his great adventure. The few existing photographs reveal that he was an extraordinary sight to behold. Most memorable was the iron mask he wore—borrowed from a suit of armor owned by Lonsdale, it weighed over four and a half pounds. Harry set off down Whitehall, pushing an enormous pram containing not a baby, but rather piles of postcards—of himself. His minder scuttled dutifully behind. It was the beginning of a long and eventful journey.

Over the next few years, the press brimmed with accounts of Harry's various exploits. At Newmarket races it was said he sold a postcard to Edward VII, though some claimed the King had asked Harry for his autograph in a cunning attempt to trick him into revealing his identity. In Kent, he was arrested for selling postcards without a license, and later appeared in full regalia before the local magistrate. After a couple of years, such was the frenzy regarding his true identity that one newspaper offered a reward of £1000 to anyone who revealed it. An enterprising chambermaid attempted to win the money by hiding under Harry's bed—but, luckily, the minder discovered her in time. Perhaps it was because of the air of mystery that surrounded him that he received countless offers of marriage, many of them from among the most titled women in Europe. The iron mask apparently had its advantages.

Over the course of the next seven years, it is said that Harry reached Australia, Canada, the United States, and possibly many other countries, and that he covered a distance of over 30,000 miles, all without ever removing his iron mask except to sleep. In August 1914, Harry reached Genoa in Italy. He had just six countries left to visit. But the arrival of a telegram at Harry's pensione brought devastating news—the outbreak of the First World War. J. P. Morgan allegedly offered Harry £4000 to settle the bet, a rather paltry sum by comparison, while other reports claim that Morgan called off the bet entirely as he was worried about the effect of the war on his financial empire. Either way, Harry had no choice but to return to England and enlist in the army.

Carbon Emissions
(or, ~~How to Murder~~ One's Grandchildren)

Most climate models show that a doubling of pre-industrial levels of greenhouse gases is very likely to commit the Earth to a rise of between 2–5° C in global mean temperatures. This level of greenhouse gases will probably be reached between 2030 and 2060. A warming of 5° C on a global scale would be far outside the realm of human experience and comparable to the difference between temperatures during the last ice age and today.

If annual greenhouse emissions remained at the current level, concentrations would be more than treble pre-industrial levels by 2100, committing the world to 3–10° C warming, based on the latest climate projections.

—The Stern Review, 2006

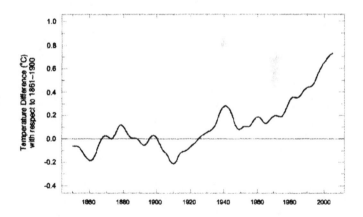

Signs of climate change are everywhere; nature is crying out for a detox. The details were recently laid out in *The Stern Review* by Sir Nicholas Stern and, evidently, the only way to help slow down the terrifying process of climate change is to reduce the amount of carbon that one's lifestyle generates. Yet it is clear from the table below that details carbon emissions caused by flights on a commercial airline from New York's JFK International Airport that just one single airplane flight has the potential to cancel out completely all of one's admirable efforts to turn off the faucet, to wear three sweaters rather than switch on the radiators, or to use energy-saving light bulbs (despite the fact that they tend to emit a not-very-cozy fluorescent glow):

Destination (from JFK)	Distance traveled in miles	Carbon dioxide emissions in tons	Percentage of total annual allowance of carbon dioxide emissions used
BOSTON, U.S.A.	380	0.1	5%
TORONTO, CANADA	732	0.2	10%
ST. LOUIS, U.S.A.	1763	0.4	20%
NASSAU, THE BAHAMAS	2193	0.5	25%
CANCUN, MEXICO	3102	0.7	35%
SAN JOSÉ, COSTA RICA	4425	0.8	40%
NUUK, GREENLAND	3703	0.9	45%

Destination (from JFK)	Distance traveled in miles	Carbon dioxide emissions in tons	Percentage of total annual allowance of carbon dioxide emissions used
Los Angeles, U.S.A.	4937	0.9	45%
London, U.K.	6886	1.2	60%
Warsaw, Poland	8510	1.5	75%
São Paulo, Brazil	9526	1.7	85%
Kahului, Hawaii	9831	1.7	85%
Buenos Aires, Argentina	10582	1.9	95%
Jerusalem, Israel	11371	2.0	100%
Tehran, Iran	12236	2.2	110%
Almaty, Kazakhstan	12712	2.3	115%
Pyongyang, North Korea	13593	2.4	120%
Nanjing, China	14698	2.6	130%
Mumbai, India	15589	2.8	140%
Manzini, Swaziland	16290	2.9	145%
Maputo, Mozambique	16372	2.9	145%

Destination (from JFK)	Distance traveled in miles	Carbon dioxide emissions in tons	Percentage of total annual allowance of carbon dioxide emissions used
PORT LOUIS, MAURITIUS	18529	3.3	165%
PERTH, AUSTRALIA	23255	4.1	205%

N. B. Figures have been calculated with reference to *The Stern Review* which suggests that, in the developed world, our carbon allowance, including both the primary carbon footprint (electricity, heating, etc.) and the secondary carbon footprint (food miles, share of public services, etc.), needs to be 2 tons per person per year (as opposed to the current figure of 9.6 tons per person per year)—that is, if human life as we know it is to have any hope at all of continuing into the next century.

N.N.B. Figures also assume that one is on a commercial airline on a direct return flight from JFK, rather than, say, a private jet, or a hang glider, or for that matter a bird, a bee, or Superman, and therefore able to fly independently, in which case different rules apply.

Ideally, we would give up flying for fun. In real life, we won't—well, not for a while anyway—and so schemes have been developed to offset carbon emissions related to flying. British Airways, for example, now makes it possible to buy carbon offsets: A return flight to Mumbai in India would cost an additional offset payment of $40 (surprisingly little), which goes toward carbon reduction projects such as greener stoves for Indian schools with which to burn crop waste, rather than discarding it.

Note, however, that these offset schemes are contentious: They may not fully compensate for the extra damage that CO_2 does to the high atmosphere, they are not always well monitored, and—above all—they help us sleep well at night when really we should be thinking about, and changing, our habits.

How to Drive in Snow

In extreme weather conditions, the best advice is: Do not drive at all. If a journey is absolutely necessary, the following advice should be heeded:

1. Before setting out, make sure you have a full tank of gas, tires in good condition, and a fully functioning car battery. Also pack basic survival equipment including water, food, a blanket, a flashlight, an ice-scraper, some antifreeze, and a shovel. A cell phone would be helpful too.

2. In icy conditions a car may require up to ten times the usual distance to stop—so adapt the distance between yourself and the car in front, and your speed, accordingly.

3. Turn on your headlights to increase the car's visibility to other motorists.

4. Use the highest gear possible to prevent wheelspin when pulling away, but when planning to turn a corner, shift into a low gear and allow the car to slow naturally before gently applying the brake.

5. Be especially careful on bridges, overpasses, and infrequently traveled roads, which freeze first.

6. If the car should start to skid, it is critical not to slam on the brakes, despite your natural reaction to do so. Instead, take your foot off the accelerator and steer into the skid, before pumping the brakes gently (i.e., by resting your heel on the floor and pumping with your toes).

7. Should the car become trapped in snow, do not spin the vehicle's wheels as this will only dig it in deeper. Instead, snow should be cleared from around the wheels by a) turning them from side to side using the steering wheel or b) using a shovel. Pouring sand, gravel, salt, or cat litter in the path of the wheels may also help improve traction. Then accelerate away gently.

Ballet

The art of dancing has ever been acknowledged to be one of the most suitable and necessary arts for physical development and for affording the primary and most natural preparation for all bodily exercises, and, among others, those concerning the use of weapons, and consequently it is one of the most valuable and useful arts for nobles and others who have the honour to enter our presence not only in time of war in our armies, but even in time of peace in our ballets.

—Louis XIV on the establishment in Paris of a Royal Academy of Music and Dance (1661)

The term "ballet" derives from the Latin verb *ballere*, meaning "to dance." Ballet originated in Italy during the Renaissance but was soon adopted with zest in France. From 1850 onward, imperial Russia became the center of the ballet world. This is reflected in the fact that today, three main methods are practiced: French, Russian, and Italian (also known as Cecchetti). The basic principles are the same, but some details differ.

THE FIVE POSITIONS OF THE FEET

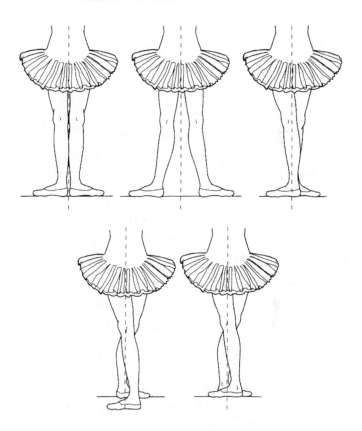

COMMONLY USED BALLET TERMS

Arabesque. A position of the body, supported on one leg with the other leg extended behind and raised. Generally used to conclude a phrase of steps.

Battement. A little like a beating action to watch, this is a step where the bent or extended leg is repeatedly raised then lowered.

Cambré. Arched, normally in relation to the shape of the body.

Chassé. Literally, chased. A step in which one foot chases the other out of its position.

Ciseaux. A scissorlike movement of the legs achieved by opening both legs into second position, either while *en pointe* or in the air.

En arrière. Backward. (Also **En devant.** In front).

En bas. Low, or when the arms are in a low position. (Also **En haut**. High, or when the arms are in a high position.)

En manège. When the dancer travels around the stage in a circular direction while performing her steps.

Entrechat. A step where the dancer leaps into the air and crosses the legs in front and behind each other in quick succession.

Echappé. An "escaping" movement—that is, when the feet are shifted from a closed to an open position, while remaining level.

Fondu(e). Describes the action of lowering the body, usually by bending the knee of the supporting leg.

Glissade. Literally, glide. An action of the foot across the floor.

Jeté. Leaping from one leg to the other, with one leg thrown to the front, side, or back.

Pas de chat. Literally, a cat's step—that is, a leap of

some kind, depending on which of the three different schools of ballet is being followed.

Pas de deux. A dance featuring two people.

Plié. A bending of the knee or knees.

Relevé. A raising of the body on pointes or demi-pointes.

BALLETS TO NOTE

The three most famous ballets in history are those composed by Tchaikovsky: *Swan Lake*, *The Nutcracker*, and *Sleeping Beauty*.

Swan Lake

Swan Lake is based on an ancient German legend. Princess Odette has been turned into a swan by an evil magician, Rothbart. The only time she reverts to human form is at midnight. To break the spell, a man who has never been in love before must fall in love with her. Then along comes Prince Siegfried. . . .

Swan Lake premiered at the Bolshoi Theatre in Moscow in 1877. The score required the full orchestral complement of strings, two flutes, two oboes, two clarinets, two bassoons, two trumpets, two cornets, three trombones, four French horns, a tuba, a harp, and—in the percussion section—a snare drum, a bass drum, a set of timpani drums, a triangle, a tambourine, symbols, castanets, a glockenspiel, and a gong. Controversy immediately surrounded the coda of the *pas de deux* between the Prince and Odette in Act III. This consists of a sequence of thirty-two *fouettes en tournant* (turns on one leg), and it was the first time that so many *fouettes* had appeared in the context of a "serious" ballet—which some saw as an amazing achievement, but others as sheer acrobatics. The feat is now a required element of every great ballerina's repertoire.

Sleeping Beauty

Inspired by the famous fairy tale, *Sleeping Beauty* is the story of the princess Aurora upon whom a spell is cast, which causes her to fall asleep for a hundred years. The only thing that can wake her is the kiss of a handsome prince. . . .

Commissioned by the director of the Imperial Theatres, the first performance was in 1890 at the Mariinsky Theatre in St. Petersburg. It was, however, something of a flop among both audiences and critics, and its genius went unrecognized until well after Tchaikovsky's death.

The Nutcracker

The Nutcracker is based on a German story called *The Nutcracker and the Mouse King* by E. T. A. Hoffmann. A young girl named Clara is given a nutcracker in the shape of a soldier for Christmas. She falls asleep, and when she wakes up, the nutcracker and all her other toys have suddenly come alive. . . .

Premiered in 1892, again at the Mariinsky Theatre, the score is very much of the Romantic period in terms of style. Also notable is the innovative use of the celesta—a cross between a glockenspiel and a piano, it had been invented just three years earlier by the Parisian harmonium builder, Auguste Mustel. Tchaikovsky employs it most memorably in the "Dance of the Sugar-Plum Fairy" in Act II.

One of the greatest versions ever of this ballet premiered in 1976 at the Kennedy Center in Washington, D.C. It was choreographed by and starred

Mikhail Baryshnikov, arguably the world's greatest (and certainly the sexiest) living dancer.

The Global AIDS Epidemic

The chart shows the estimated percentage of the adult population (aged 15–49) with HIV.

COUNTRY/REGION	ESTIMATE
Sub-Saharan Africa	
Angola	3.7
Benin	1.8
Botswana	24.1
Burkina Faso	2.0
Burundi	3.3
Cameroon	5.4
Central African Republic	10.7
Chad	3.5
Comoros	< 0.1
Congo	5.3
Côte d'Ivoire	7.1
Democratic Republic of Congo	3.2
Djibouti	3.1
Equatorial Guinea	3.2
Eritrea	2.4
Ethiopia	n/a
Gabon	7.9
Gambia	2.4
Ghana	2.3
Guinea	1.5
Guinea-Bissau	3.8
Kenya	6.1

Country/Region	Estimate
Lesotho	23.2
Liberia	n/a
Madagascar	0.5
Malawi	14.1
Mali	1.7
Mauritania	0.7
Mauritius	0.6
Mozambique	16.1
Namibia	19.6
Niger	1.1
Nigeria	3.9
Rwanda	3.1
Senegal	0.9
Sierra Leone	1.6
Somalia	0.9
South Africa	18.8
Swaziland	33.4
Togo	3.2
Uganda	6.7
United Republic of Tanzania	6.5
Zambia	17.0
Zimbabwe	20.1

East Asia

China	0.1
Democratic People's Republic of Korea	n/a
Japan	< 0.1
Mongolia	< 0.1
Republic of Korea	< 0.1

Country/Region	Estimate
Oceania	
Australia	0.1
Fiji	0.1
New Zealand	0.1
Papua New Guinea	1.8
South and Southeast Asia	
Afghanistan	< 0.1
Bangladesh	< 0.1
Bhutan	< 0.1
Brunei Darussalam	< 0.1
Cambodia	1.6
India	0.9
Indonesia	0.1
Iran	0.2
Lao People's Democratic Republic	0.1
Malaysia	0.5
Maldives	n/a
Myanmar	1.3
Nepal	0.5
Pakistan	0.1
Philippines	< 0.1
Singapore	0.3
Sri Lanka	< 0.1
Thailand	1.4
Timor-Leste	n/a
Vietnam	0.5

Country/Region	Estimate
Eastern Europe and Central Asia	
Armenia	0.1
Azerbaijan	0.1
Belarus	0.3
Bosnia and Herzegovina	< 0.1
Bulgaria	< 0.1
Croatia	< 0.1
Estonia	1.3
Georgia	0.2
Kazakhstan	0.1
Kyrgyzstan	0.1
Latvia	0.8
Lithuania	0.2
Republic of Moldova	1.1
Romania	< 0.1
Russian Federation	1.1
Tajikistan	0.1
Turkmenistan	< 0.1
Ukraine	1.4
Uzbekistan	0.2
Western and Central Europe	
Albania	< 0.2
Austria	0.3
Belgium	0.3
Czech Republic	0.1
Denmark	0.2
Finland	0.1
France	0.4

Country/Region	Estimate
Germany	0.1
Greece	0.2
Hungary	0.1
Iceland	0.2
Ireland	0.2
Italy	0.5
Luxembourg	0.2
Malta	0.1
Netherlands	0.2
Norway	0.1
Poland	0.1
Portugal	0.4
Serbia and Montenegro	0.2
Slovakia	< 0.1
Slovenia	< 0.1
Spain	0.6
Sweden	0.2
Switzerland	0.4
(The former Yugoslav Republic of) Macedonia	< 0.1
United Kingdom of Great Britain and Northern Ireland	0.2

North Africa and Middle East

Algeria	0.1
Bahrain	n/a
Cyprus	n/a
Egypt	< 0.1
Iraq	n/a
Israel	n/a

Country/Region	Estimate
Jordan	n/a
Kuwait	n/a
Lebanon	0.1
Libyan Arab Jamahiriya	n/a
Morocco	0.1
Oman	n/a
Qatar	n/a
Saudi Arabia	n/a
Sudan	1.6
Syrian Arab Republic	n/a
Tunisia	0.1
Turkey	n/a
United Arab Emirates	n/a
Yemen	n/a

North America

Canada	0.3
United States of America	0.6

Caribbean

Bahamas	3.3
Barbados	1.5
Cuba	0.1
Dominican Republic	1.1
Haiti	3.8
Jamaica	1.5
Trinidad and Tobago	2.6

Country/Region	Estimate
Latin America	
Argentina	0.6
Belize	2.5
Bolivia	0.1
Brazil	0.5
Chile	0.3
Colombia	0.6
Costa Rica	0.3
Ecuador	0.3
El Salvador	0.9
Guatemala	0.9
Guyana	2.4
Honduras	1.5
Mexico	0.3
Nicaragua	0.2
Panama	0.9
Paraguay	0.4
Peru	0.6
Suriname	1.9
Uruguay	0.5
Venezuela	0.7

Source: 2006 Report on the global AIDS epidemic, May 2006, U.N.A.I.D.S.

How to Eat a Pineapple

"And as the race of pine-apples, so is the race of man."
—*William Makepeace Thackeray*, Pendennis, *1850*

For those who have not tasted a pineapple for a while, a revisit of this fabulously exotic fruit is highly recommended. Since the emergence in the 1990s of a new variety known as the Gold, they are more delicious than they once were—sweeter, less acidic, and less fibrous—as well as more nutritious, containing over four times the previous level of Vitamin C.

Do not be deterred by the admittedly challenging task of ascertaining whether or not a particular specimen is ripe. Smell it, then ensure the leaves are green, the thorny "eyes" are brown, and the base gives a little when squished. Bear in mind that the color of the rind is the least reliable indicator.

To prepare a pineapple, first slice off the crown and the base. Then, holding the fruit upright, slice the skin off in vertical sections all the way around. A few "eyes" will be left—gouge these out with a knife (the tip of a potato peeler works even more efficiently). With the fruit still upright, slice it in half lengthways and in half again, then remove the core (this is actually the continuation of the fruit's stalk, which is why it is sometimes a little chewy).

The pineapple is originally from South America, and native tribes in Peru ate it chopped into small pieces and soaked in water and salt; in Colombia and Venezuela, it was boiled with manioc starch for breakfast, while the Caribs of Guadeloupe, which is where Christopher Columbus first stumbled across the fruit in 1493, used a mortar to pound the fruit into a thick paste, then seasoned it with capiscum peppers. It was not until centuries later, however, that the first official written recipes featuring the fruit began to appear. . . .

FIVE RECIPES FEATURING A PINEAPPLE

To make a Tart of the Ananas, or Pine-Apple. From Barbados. Take a Pine-Apple, and twist off its Crown: then pare it free from the Knots, and cut it in Slices about half an inch thick; then stew it with a little Canary Wine, or Madera Wine, and some Sugar, till it is thoroughly hot, and it will distribute its Flavor to the Wine much better than any thing we can add to it. When it is as one would have it, take it from the Fire; and when it is cool, put it into a sweet Paste, with its Liquor, and bake it gently a little while, and when it comes from the Oven, pour Cream over it (if you have it) and serve it either hot or cold.

—A recipe for a pineapple tart from The Country Housewife by Richard Bradley (1732)

Pare your pine-apples, and cut them in thin round slices. Weigh the slices, and to each pound allow a pound of loaf-sugar. Dissolve the sugar in a very small quantity of water, stir it, and set it over the fire in a preserving-kettle. Boil it ten minutes, skimming it well. Then put in it the pine-apple slices, and boil them till they are clear and soft, but not until they break. About half an hour (or perhaps less time) will suffice. Let them cool in a large dish or pan, before you put them in their jars, which you must do carefully, lest they break. Pour the syrup over them. Tie them up with brandy paper.

—A recipe for preserved pineapple from Seventy-Five Receipts for Pastry, Cakes and Sweet-meats by Eliza Leslie (1828)

Ingredients—A small pineapple, a small wineglassful of brandy or liqueur, 2 oz. of sifted sugar, batter . . .

Mode—. . . Pare the pine with as little waste as possible, cut it into rather thin slices, and soak these slices in the above proportion of brandy or liqueur and pounded sugar for 4 hours; then make a batter . . .; and, when this is ready, dip in the pieces of pine, and fry them in boiling lard from 5 to 8 minutes; turn them from the lard before the fire, dish them on a white d'oyley, strew over them sifted sugar, and serve quickly.

—A recipe for pineapple fritters from The Book of Household Management *by Mrs. Beeton (1861)*

Preheat oven to 400 degrees. Then for each pound of canned baked beans, stir in 2 tbsp brown sugar, 1 tbsp syrup drained from Dole Pineapple slices, 1 tbsp catsup and 1 tbsp prepared mustard. Bake for 30 minutes, then top with drained Dole Pineapple slices and bake for 30 minutes more. Elegant enough to serve company—easy enough to fix just for the family!

—A recipe for canned pineapple with baked beans by the Dole Corporation's in-house home economist (1958)

INGREDIENTS:
1 ripe pineapple
Demerara sugar, enough to fill a shallow dish
7 ounces dark chocolate
Half a cup of Malibu rum
2 tablespoons caster sugar (depending on
    the bitterness of the chocolate)
Half a cup of double cream

Soak some bamboo skewers in water for 20 minutes.

*Cut the top and bottom off the pineapple, and working
vertically slice the skin off the fruit.*

*Cut into quarters and then into about three pieces
again lengthways so that you have wedges of pineapple,
cut off the woody core.*

*Thread the wedges onto the soaked bamboo skewers
lengthways and lay in a shallow dish.*

*Put the chocolate broken up into pieces, into a thick-
bottomed pan with the Malibu, sugar and cream and melt
over a low heat. Then pour the sauce into dipping bowls.*

*Meanwhile, either grill or barbecue the pineapple,
dredging it in Demerara sugar first, until it caramelizes
in the heat.*

*Dip the pineapple skewers into the hot chocolate sauce
and eat.*

—*A recipe for caramelized pineapple with hot chocolate
sauce from* Forever Summer *by Nigella Lawson
(2003). Bliss.*

What to Drink When

In the country: A pint of ale is a must (even if some
of it ends up left in the glass to get warm). A hearty
walk beforehand is the best way to work up a thirst.
Wherever possible, sample the joys of the local brewery
or microbrewery. It can be an acquired taste, but
persevere, since all ales have different characteristics;
one is sure to find a brew that suits eventually.

Girls' night out: Terribly outmoded until recently,
rosé wine is now considered perfectly respectable, even
chic. On the whole, the drier styles are far superior—
the French and Portuguese tend to do these best.
For the height of luxury, Krug Rosé Champagne is
unsurpassed.

Alone in a bar: Not straight spirits, as this suggests a woman on the brink. For those who wish to be left alone, a glass of red wine is suitably neutral. In the post-smoking age, meanwhile, one must confine one's attention to a good book. Failing that, zip around the corner to buy a newspaper (never resort to a cell phone—terribly gauche).

Hot date: Whiskey never fails to impress. Scotch single malts are preferable—for extra cachet choose a peaty one from Islay (pronounced "eye-lah"), as these are generally considered too challenging for female palates. But ensure you have the pronunciation correct before you order, for example, Bruichladdich ("brook-laddie"), Laphroaig ("lah-froig"), or Bunnahabhain ("boo-na-ha-venn").

With the in-laws: Not a beer—in their day, women only drank beer if they were alcoholics or loose. Go for something suitably neutral like a gin and tonic instead.

In a fabulous bar: Be adventurous. If in doubt, ask the bartender to advise—they long to be asked, and may even provide a free tasting opportunity if business is slow. Fashionable spirits at present include gin, rum, and tequila.

At Christmas: Mulled wine. Any excuse.

With the church choir: Sweet sherry.

With a Japanese businessman: Scotch single malt whiskey (it is incredibly expensive in Japan).

In a Spanish finca at about 6:30 p.m. in July: Cold, dry sherry.

On reaching the North Pole: Zubrowka bison grass vodka mixed with apple juice. A vastly underrated drink.

In a time machine on the way to nineteenth-century

Paris accompanied by Toulouse-Lautrec and three prostitutes: Absinthe. In no other circumstances is this an acceptable tipple.

How to Put Up a Tent in the Dark

The most important step of all when putting up a tent in the dark is to remember to take the thing with you in the first place. Checking that you have the full complement of tent poles and pegs before you leave is also advisable; otherwise, it is not uncommon to be forced into one of two scenarios, both equally unsatisfactory:

a) bivouac in
   something like this

or

b) sleep with something
   like this

Indeed, it is advisable to practice putting up your tent in the daylight, and somewhere dry, before beginning a camping trip in order to avoid the pitfalls outlined below.

Figuring out which part of a tent goes where has the potential to be infuriatingly confusing. As a result, many modern manufacturers now include a color-coded system to help. But you will not be able to see this as it will be dark. It may also be raining, so it is essential to take plenty of trash bags to cover your possessions and your companions while they sit waiting on the wet grass.

Throughout the process, it is advisable to try not to lose one's temper, as even poles that have been designed for camping on Everest suddenly bend at right angles in the hands of an angry camper. Ditto tent pegs, if there are any left by this stage. If there are not, steal them from the tent next door.

It is important that the fly sheet (that is, the second layer that goes on top) is kept taut and that it does not touch the main body of the tent, as this will alter the surface tension and cause a leak, followed by a kerfuffle. Securely pinned guy ropes will help to maintain this structure; but they will also trip up drunken passersby in the night, endangering the safety of the tent's inhabitants, so beware.

Some people try to make camping more fun by having a designer tent that is decorated with pictures of flowers or animals. This is a fruitless strategy, and is to be avoided, since dressing things up to be something other than they are is never advisable—not even when the tent in question is designed by Cath Kidston.

The most useful piece of advice when putting up a tent in the dark is to do it adorned in a gorgeous pair of Wellington boots. If decorated ridiculously enough, they have the wonderful effect of making even the most reluctant camper feel instantly twelve years old again. Ironically, Cath Kidston (www.cathkidston.com) does a fabulous line in decorated wellies. Alternatively, seek out a pair of Hunters for the best-made boots of this type.

The Constellations

Star light, star bright
The first star I see tonight,
I wish I may, I wish I might,
Have the wish I wish tonight.

—*Nineteenth-century nursery rhyme by Mother Goose*
(later borrowed by Madonna for her song "Lucky Star")

The arrangement of the stars has remained basically the same at least since written records began. A list compiled by the Greek astronomer Hipparchus in about 120 B.C. confirms this—the pattern is the same, as is the brightness, and they are even in almost the same place. Today the sky is (somewhat arbitrarily) divided into eighty-eight different groups of stars, each of which is known as a constellation. Especially significant are the constellations that lie along the ecliptic, which is the path the Sun appears to trace across the sky in the course of the earth's yearly cycle (in scientific terms, this is the plane defined by the earth's orbit around the Sun). These constellations are known as the signs of the zodiac. To identify a constellation, one must imagine lines drawn between each star—though, even then, few bear much resemblance to the mythical or semimythical beings after which most of them are named. Three of the easiest to spot from the Northern Hemisphere are as follows.

ORION

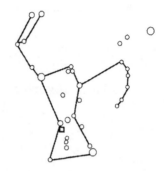

Visible from approximately October to March. Named after a giant hunter of Greek mythology. The key to finding him is to search the sky for his belt—three stars of similar brightness in a row in the middle of the constellation. Just below, look for his sword. Orion also contains a deep sky object visible to the naked eye called the Orion Nebula, which is a massive cloud of gases and dust where new stars are born.

URSA MAJOR

Latin for Great Bear, the other name by which it is commonly known. In the Marshall Islands it is called the

Canoe, and in Arab countries the Funeral Bier (a frame for carrying a coffin); in ancient Egypt it was believed to depict a thigh. Regardless, this is the constellation that also features the famous Big Dipper. Made up of seven main stars, the Big Dipper can be identified by looking north, then either just to the left or the right.

URSA MINOR

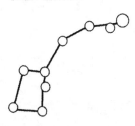

Latin for Little Bear. At the very end of the bear's long tail, look for Polaris, also known as the North Star or the Pole Star—located directly above the North Pole. For centuries it has been used by travelers to figure out which way is north (a fact to be borne in mind when en route to a mini-break in the Great Lakes). In Norse mythology, it is the jewel on the end of a spike the gods stuck through the universe, around which the sky revolves.

Of the other eighty-five constellations, 32% are named after inanimate objects, 23% after land animals, 16% after men and women, 11% after water creatures, 10% after birds, 4% after mythical creatures, 2% after insects, 1% after a geographical feature, and 1% after someone's hair. An excellent reminder of the important things in life—compasses, unicorns, and air pumps—they are also a rather good source of out-of-the-ordinary baby names.

Name	Meaning
Andromeda	Chained maiden
Antlia	Air pump[1]
Apus	Bird of paradise
Aquarius	Water bearer
Aquila	Eagle
Ara	Altar
Aries	Ram
Auriga	Charioteer
Boötes	Herdsmen
Caelum	Chisel
Camelopardalis	Giraffe
Cancer	Crab
Canes Venatici	Hunting dogs
Canis Major	Greater dog
Canis Minor	Littler dog
Capricornus	Sea-goat
Carina	Keel
Cassiopeia	Queen
Centaurus	Centaur
Cepheus	King
Cetus	Whale
Chamaeleon	Chameleon
Circinus	Drawing compass
Columba	Dove
Coma Berenices	Berenice's hair[2]

---

1 Named after an air pump invented by the British chemist and physicist Robert Boyle (1627–1691).

2 Named after Berenice (c. 273-221 B.C.), the beautiful wife of the ancient Egyptian king Ptolemy III. She promised to sacrifice her long blond hair to the goddess Aphrodite if her husband returned safely from battle. He did, so her hair was deposited in the temple. When it

Name	Meaning
Corona Australis	Southern crown
Corona Borealis	Northern crown
Corvus	Crow
Crater	Cup
Crux	Cross
Cygnus	Swan
Delphinus	Dolphin
Dorado	Goldfish
Draco	Dragon
Equuleus	Little horse
Eridanus	River
Formax	Furnace
Gemini	Twins
Grus	Crane
Hercules	Hercules
Horologium	Clock
Hydra	Female water snake
Hydrus	Male water snake
Indus	Indian
Lacerta	Lizard
Leo	Lion
Leo Minor	Lion cub
Lepus	Hare
Libra	Balance
Lupus	Wolf
Lynx	Lynx
Lyra	Lyre

---

disappeared a few days later, the king was about to condemn the temple guards to death when the court astronomer declared that, in fact, Aphrodite had been so delighted with Berenice's present that she had placed it in the sky for everyone to admire for all eternity.

Name	Meaning
Mensa	Table mountain
Microscopium	Microscope
Monoceros	Unicorn
Musca	Fly
Norma	Square
Octans	Octant
Ophiuchus	Serpent bearer
Pavo	Peacock
Pegasus	Flying horse
Perseus	Hero
Phoenix	Phoenix
Pictor	Painter
Pisces	Fishes
Piscis Austrinus	Southern fish
Puppis	Stern (of a ship)
Pyxis	Sea compass
Reticulum	Reticle[3]
Sagitta	Arrow
Sagittarius	Archer
Scorpius	Scorpion
Sculptor	Sculptor
Scutum	Shield
Serpens	Serpent
Sextans	Sextant
Taurus	Bull
Telescopium	Telescope
Triangulum	Triangle
Triangulum Australe	Southern triangle

3   Named after the grid of fine lines in a telescope eyepiece that helps to center and focus.

Name	Meaning
Tucana	Toucan
Vela	Sail
Virgo	Maiden
Volans	Flying fish
Vulpecula	Fox

All are best viewed on a clear, cold night, dressed in a big coat and hat and gloves, clutching a bottle of champagne in one hand and a lover in the other.

Major Foreign Aid Donors

	As a percentage of the Gross National Income	In millions of U.S. dollars
Norway	0.87	2,199
Denmark	0.85	2,037
Luxembourg	0.83	236
Sweden	0.78	2,722
Netherlands	0.73	4,204
Portugal	0.63	1,031
France	0.41	8,473
Switzerland	0.41	1,545
Belgium	0.41	1,463
Ireland	0.39	607
United Kingdom	0.36	7,883
Finland	0.35	655
Germany	0.28	7,534

	As a percentage of the Gross National Income	In millions of U.S. dollars
Canada	0.27	2,599
Australia	0.25	1,460
Spain	0.24	2,437
Austria	0.23	678
Greece	0.23	465
New Zealand	0.23	212
Japan	0.19	8,906
United States	0.17	19,705
Italy	0.15	2,462

Source: Organization for Economic Cooperation and Development Factbook 2006.

New Year's Eve

Only the peculiar or deluded actually enjoy New Year's Eve. The rest of us simply bear it as best we can. There is no doubt that it helps to be somewhere other than within a fifty-mile radius of one's usual stomping ground, and ideally abroad—Rome, perhaps, or Cancun. This makes going to an overpriced restaurant, elbowing one's way into a local bar, crashing the party of someone one doesn't know and then trudging through the streets at 7 a.m. in search of a taxicab seem glamorous, rather than nightmarish. Another tip is to learn to play *Auld Lang Syne* on an instrument of your choice, solving forever the perennial problem of not having anyone to kiss when the bells strike midnight.

AULD LANG SYNE

Music: traditional, lyrics: Robert Burns

Auld Lang Syne

Tattoos[1]

A practice originally known as "pricking," tattooing only really became fashionable after 1862 when the Prince of Wales (the future Edward VII) was inspired by a visit to Jerusalem to have the image of the Jerusalem Cross tattooed on his arm. Early forms of tattooing employed combs, chisels, or rakes to puncture the skin before adding the pigment. Some tribes in the Arctic used a needle threaded with soot-coated yarn. Methods have, however, moved on a little since then.

The tattoo machine as we know it was invented by an Irish-American named Samuel O'Reilly in 1891. It was based on an engraving machine invented some years earlier by Thomas Edison. The machine, the design of which has changed little since then, is a kind of drill, a bit like the one the dentist uses (the two sound identical, in fact). The drill uses a needle to puncture the skin by about a millimeter, thousands of times a minute. With each puncture, one drop of insoluble ink is injected into the dermis—the second layer of the skin after the epidermis, which is the outer layer.

Some describe the pain experienced when getting a tattoo as akin to the pain of a bee sting, pins and needles, or being pinched. They are lying. Getting a tattoo is, after childbirth, among the single most painful experiences known to the human race. Indeed, many react in a similar way—screaming, crying, swearing, or wishing it was over instantly. To this end, do not be

---

1   Other words beginning with the letters "tatt" include:
      • **tatterdemalion** (*adj.*, raggedly dressed and unkempt; *noun*, somebody wearing ragged clothes)
      • **tattersall** (*noun*, a pattern of squares or checks formed by dark lines on a light or brightly colored background)
      • **tatting** (*noun*, a form of lace made with a shuttle)
      • **tattle** (*verb*, to gossip about other people's secrets)

overambitious in the choice of design. The larger the design, the longer the pain endured. Also, take a friend who is good at bullying you—or, even better, an acquaintance in front of whom you are reluctant to appear a coward. An ex-paramour also works well in this capacity.

Either way, it is imperative that the choice of location for the tattoo is dictated by one's personal pain threshold. The closer it is to a bone, the thinner the skin and the closer the nerves are to the surface; therefore, the more it will hurt. It is not wise to take a preventative aspirin beforehand: this will simply thin the blood, with the result that one bleeds more and the process takes longer.

TATTOO LOCATION IN RELATION TO PAIN THRESHOLD

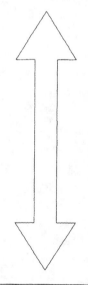

High Pain Threshold

Ankle (too painful due to
proximity to bone)

Along the spine (ditto)

Neck (ditto)

Inside of the arm

Ribs

Hands

Feet

Outside of the arms

Shoulders

Back

Low Pain Threshold

- **tattler** (*noun*, somebody who gossips about other people's secrets; a long-legged shore bird that is related to sandpipers and is noted for its loud cries)
- **tattletale grey** (*adj.*, of a white color with a grey tinge)
- **tatty** (*adj.*, shabby, run-down, or in poor condition)

Other tattoo locations to be discouraged are: the breast (risk of sagging), the upper thigh (ditto), the stomach (ditto, as well as risk of stretching during pregnancy), and the face (obviously). In other words, any body part that is likely to change much in the course of a lifetime is to be avoided. Also bear in mind issues of visibility. How easy would it be to cover it up with a Band-Aid at a job interview, Sunday brunch with the in-laws, or coffee with the pastor?

Even more crucial is the choice of design. For those keen to make a statement, entire body tattoos are becoming increasingly popular—sometimes with some plastic surgery to create a bifurcated tongue thrown in. For the less committed, try to dream up something that will retain its appeal even when you are 105 and spending your days drinking laudanum straight from the bottle. So, for a cellist, a drawing of a pair of F-holes on your lower back might be a suitable adornment, while those with a passion for tortoises or a penchant for apples could consider these as options. If your dream is to have the name of a loved one tattooed on some part of you, ensure that in the event of a change of circumstances, it has the potential to be modified without too much trouble or trauma. The name Francesca, for instance, could in theory be adapted to read "France," "frantic," "frank," or even "frangible" (meaning "capable of being broken or damaged"). This works better with some names than others. So if your lover is a Ben, Dan, or Sam, then go ahead, tattoo away; if he is a Sebastian, Muhammad, or Reginald, caution is recommended.

Shoes

*I think that when you get dressed in the morning, sometimes you're
really making a decision about your behavior for the day.
Like if you put on flip-flops, you're saying: "I hope I don't
get chased today." "Be nice to people in sneakers."*

—Demetri Martin (American comedian, b.1973)

A battle between high heels and kitten heels raged for
some years, but, thankfully, the latter have now been
vanquished once and for all, relegated to their proper
place as a late 1990s/early 2000s relic. The fatal flaw
with the entire concept of kitten heels had always been
that if a woman wanted to be comfortable, she might as
well wear a lovely pair of flats. Why wobble around on
a tiny spike that is only an inch high? If one is going
to bother to wobble, wobble big, and ensure one's
legs look longer in the process. Thus, high—really
high—heels have won their rightful place as the master
adorner of women's feet.

High heels do present a number of practical problems
to any woman who is not: a) a celebrity b) a millionairess
or c) any other kind of being who travels only in taxis,
rather than one who takes the train or bus, or who trudges
half a mile in the rain while trying to decipher a splattered
printout of a street map, like the rest of womankind; yet
there is a solution. Wear high heels, but carry a pair of
flip-flops in your handbag at all times. (In winter, replace
flip-flops with bendable sneakers). Simply change when
near your destination. (The key is not to get caught mid-
change, so embark upon the foot revamp not on the
doorstep, but a couple of streets away at least.) Then one

can run for a bus *and* sashay like Marilyn Monroe all in the course of a single day. Hurrah.

Shoes are one of the few products where one *does* get what one pays for. This applies to high heels in particular—the more expensive they are, the more comfortable they are to walk in and the longer they last. As a result, they are one item upon which it is worth frittering away a fair bit of cash. To this end, try as often as possible to wear shoes to have adventures in, to paraphrase Vivienne Westwood.

SHOES TO HAVE ADVENTURES IN

Perfect for skipping down the boardwalk at Cannes.

Just right for a country fair. There is no danger of sinking into the grass in these, nor encountering any broken glass that may be strewn about.

These moc-croc sneakers are destined for the final day of New York Fashion Week: In what other apparel can one expect to be able to race all over town, yet maintain the glamour that such an occasion demands?

Ugg boots are perfect for . . . nothing and nowhere. Worn for more than a day, one simply ends up with athlete's foot and a fatted calf—yours, not the farmer's.

Ideal when pregnant, yet stubbornly refusing to look like a frump. Vintage shoes are an excellent way of picking up classic, high-end collectibles. All being well, they will not have molded to the shape of their previous owner (who may have died. Wearing them. Such shoes are not for the squeamish).

Perfect for any event that does not actually involve standing up. This $10 job from Payless is only for the iron-footed: mostly crafted from a hard generation of plastic, it is a shoe that seems to be designed for something far more industrial than mere human feet.

1. Take small steps (pencil skirts give one a natural advantage because they force one to—Marilyn Monroe was no dumb blonde, it turns out).

2. Swing the hips.

3. Never, ever look back.

Animal Stings, Bites, or Otherwise Unfriendly Approaches

With adventures come dangers—which should not put one off, but simply be borne in mind. When trouble of the animal variety arises, the optimum solution in most cases is to scream and shout, and seek professional help immediately. However, there are scenarios in which screaming and shouting will prove useless. So it is best to be prepared. Do not bother to look for Indiana Jones; he is never there when needed. *Be* Indiana Jones. In any case, an alligator attack is not to be tolerated—unless one is carrying an alligator skin bag, in which case the poor creature has a point.

(In all cases of bites and stings, keep an eye out for signs of anaphylactic shock—wheezing, difficulty swallowing, a much-increased heart rate, swelling or itching anywhere other than the wound—because this can be fatal. At this point, professional medical attention definitely needs to be sought, and fast.)

Attacker	BEE OR WASP
How to avoid	Do not wear brightly colored or patterned clothes that to a bee might look like a flower patch. In the case of both bees and wasps, if one does land, stand still. Do not frighten it. Do not make rapid movements. Blow on it gently to move it along. (See also page 40.)
What to do if attacked	Remove the stinger with your fingers, trying not to spread the venom further under the skin as you do so. The pain will only increase if in the process you manage to puncture the bee stinger's venomous sac. Remove it as quickly as possible because the venom continues to enter the skin for up to sixty seconds after the initial sting. Wash the affected area with soap and water, then raise it to prevent swelling and cover with a cold washcloth. Apply antihistamine, if available, to relieve the itching, then swallow some painkillers.

Attacker	DOG OR CAT
How to avoid	Be kind.
What to do if attacked	Wash wound with soap and water. Elevate to above the level of the heart to inhibit swelling and avoid infection. Apply pressure with a clean, dry cloth to stop the bleeding, then bandage. Should the bite occur in a country where rabies remains a possibility, it is vital that a vaccination be administered.

Attacker	SPIDER OR SCORPION
How to avoid	Avoid damp, dark areas, where spiders like to lurk. Check luggage because scorpions are famous for their stowaway antics.
What to do if attacked	Scrape off the stinger with a credit card or something similar. Apply ice for ten minutes, remove for ten minutes—this is to prevent tissue damage as a result of keeping the ice on too long—then repeat.

Attacker	JELLYFISH, CORAL, OR ANEMONE
How to avoid	Look out for them when swimming. All sting when disturbed.
What to do if attacked	Rinse the wound with salt water (not fresh water which will only intensify the pain). If stung by a jellyfish and the tentacles are still wrapped around the affected area, remove them, but be careful—wear gloves or use tweezers. Soak the wound for at least half an hour to neutralize the toxins in the tentacles. Anything acidic will work: urine is one option, but it does not contain enough acid to be particularly effective, so vinegar is preferable. Restrict the movement of the affected area to ensure the venom does not spread too much. Clean with disinfectant. Take painkillers.

Attacker	BEDBUG
How to avoid	Move the bed well away from the wall. Leave a light on. Wash the bedsheets in hot water.

What to do if attacked	Take an antihistamine; painkiller pills; apply hydrocortisone cream: all will help relieve the horrid itching.

Attacker	STINGRAY
How to avoid	It hates to be surprised, and stings to scare you away. To avoid being stung, shuffle your feet along the seabed to warn any that are lurking that you're approaching—though be careful not to stub your toe, which can be pretty darned painful in itself.
What to do if attacked	Control any bleeding. Use clean, fresh water and some soap to clean the wound. The removal of the stinger causes severe bleeding, so ideally, leave the stinger until emergency care arrives. If care is not going to arrive for ages, remove any leftover parts of the stinger with tweezers. Never remove it from the chest or abdomen, though. Neutralize the toxin by immersing the wound in hot, fresh water.

Attacker	WEEVER FISH
How to avoid	A small sand-colored fish that buries itself in the sand on the seabed. In order to avoid, look out for the spines on its back. These contain venom so if you step on them, it will hurt considerably.
What to do if attacked	Remove the spines with tweezers. Wash the affected area, in the hottest water you can tolerate, for about half an hour—this helps destroy the venom.

Attacker	TICK
How to avoid	Wear long sleeves and trousers. Spray on repellent . . . blah blah blah—once the critters decide they are going to cause trouble, there is little one can do about it except submit to the whim of these insidious pests.
What to do if attacked	Use tweezers to remove the tick—but use constant, gentle pressure; otherwise you'll tear the creature in half and some will be left behind in the wound. Do not twist or jerk it out or try to burn it out. Examine the tick to ensure it has indeed all been removed. Disinfect.

Attacker	ALLIGATOR
How to avoid	Avoid lakes and rivers in tropical climates.
What to do if attacked	Run or swim away using whatever means possible; but if cornered, try to get on its back and push down on its neck to force the jaw down. Attack its eyes and nose with any weapon, even your fist. If it does manage to bite you, tap it on the nose. This often makes it open up its jaws again, which will allow you to escape. Go to a hospital.

Attacker	LION
How to avoid	Steer clear of the Gir Forest in northwest India and reserves and national parks south of the Sahara desert in Africa.

What to do if attacked	Do not run. Talk to the lion in a calm but firm voice. Make yourself appear larger than you are—raise your arms or open your jacket out. Try to move backward slowly, but do not turn your back on it. Do not make sudden movements. The aim is to convince the lion that you are not prey, but rather a danger. Fight back with rocks, sticks, or anything available.
Attacker	SHARK
How to avoid	Steer clear of the kinds of environments that attract a hungry shark—the mouth of a river after heavy rain; anywhere near a fishing boat; anywhere near large groups of sea lions, seals, dolphins, or fish; anywhere near dead animals; anywhere near sewage; murky waters; the entrance to a harbor; or anywhere you see fish or turtles behaving oddly. Do not wear orange or yellow or fancy jewelry that might look like fish scales. Do not splash about too much.
What to do if attacked	Get out of the water as quickly as possible. Control the bleeding by applying pressure to the wound. Remove any fragments of teeth or debris left in the wound. Keep warm. Do not move without good reason. Wash with soap and water and then bandage. Go to a hospital.

Attacker	HUMAN

How to avoid   Be kind.

What to do   Can be more dangerous than animal bites
if attacked   because the human mouth is even more of
a hotbed of different types of viruses and
bacteria. Apply pressure on the wound with
a clean, dry cloth to stop the bleeding. Wash
with soap and water, then apply disinfectant.
Wrap some ice in a wet cloth and apply it to the
wound to relieve the pain (applying it directly
might freeze the skin). Then bandage.[1]

The Approximate Caloric Value of Various Foodstuffs

An apple	*72 calories*
A banana	*105 calories*
A Mars Bar	*230 calories*
A bowl of cornflakes with skim milk	*200 calories*
A chrysanthemum leaf	*4 calories*
A kumquat	*13 calories*
An ounce of raw acorns	*109 calories*
1 pound of body fat tissue	*3,500 calories*
A glass of champagne	*89 calories*
A pint of Guinness	*170 calories*
A fistful of candy on Halloween	*200 calories*

---

1   Unless it is a love bite—in which case, ignore all the given advice,
giggle, and congratulate yourself at still having the love life of a teen-
ager. Then apply some toothpaste.

A portion of nachos with cheese and jalapeño peppers	*600 calories*
A Dungeness crab (cooked)	*94 calories*
An entire medium-size roast turkey, with the skin	*2,142 calories*
65 hard boiled eggs eaten in 6 minutes, 40 seconds, which is the world record for competitive eating held by Sonya Thomas, a 39-year-old woman from Virginia (who weighs, incidentally, just 105 pounds)	*5,005 calories*
4.18400 joules, which is the quantity of thermal energy required to raise 1g of water by 1°C at 15°C [1]	*1 calorie*

Nobel Peace Prize Winners

2006	Muhammad Yunus, Grameen Bank
2005	Mohamed ElBaradei, International Atomic Energy Agency
2004	Wangari Maathai[2] ♠
2003	Shirin Ebadi[3] ♠
2002	Jimmy Carter
2001	Kofi Annan, United Nations
2000	Kim Dae-jung
1999	Médecins Sans Frontières
1998	John Hume, David Trimble

---

1 Also the definition of the term "calorie," which comes from the Latin for "heat," calor.

2 Born and based in Kenya, Maathai won for her contributions to democracy, human rights, and, in particular, environmental conservation.

3 A lawyer from Iran, Ebadi has dedicated her life to fighting for the rights of women and children.

1997	Jody Williams[4] ♣, International Campaign to Ban Landmines
1996	Carlos Filipe Ximenes Belo, José Ramos-Horta
1995	Joseph Rotblat, Pugwash Conferences on Science and World Affairs
1994	Yasser Arafat, Shimon Peres, Yitzhak Rabin
1993	Nelson Mandela, F. W. de Klerk
1992	Rigoberta Menchú Tum[5] ♣
1991	Aung San Suu Kyi[6] ♣
1990	Mikhail Gorbachev
1989	The fourteenth Dalai Lama
1988	United Nations Peacekeeping Forces
1987	Oscar Arias Sánchez
1986	Elie Wiesel
1985	International Physicians for the Prevention of Nuclear War
1984	Desmond Tutu
1983	Lech Walesa
1982	Alva Myrdal[7] ♣, Alfonso García Robles
1981	Office of the United Nations High Commissioner for Refugees
1980	Adolfo Pérez Esquivel
1979	Mother Teresa[8] ♣

---

4 Awarded the prize for her work campaigning against landmines.

5 Born in Guatemala, Menchú won in recognition of her work promoting the rights of the indigenous people of Central America.

6 Won for her nonviolent struggle to establish a democratic government in Burma (also known as Myanmar) which is still governed by a military junta today.

7 An advocate of disarmament.

8 Originally from Macedonia, Mother Teresa's work with the very poor, in particular in Calcutta, is well known.

1978	Anwar al-Sadat, Menachem Begin
1977	Amnesty International
1976	Betty Williams, Mairead Corrigan[9] ♦ ♦
1975	Andrei Sakharov
1974	Seán MacBride, Eisaku Sato
1973	Henry Kissinger, Le Duc Tho
1972	No prize awarded
1971	Willy Brandt
1970	Norman Borlaug
1969	International Labour Organization
1968	René Cassin
1967	No prize awarded
1966	No prize awarded
1965	United Nations Children's Fund
1964	Martin Luther King
1963	International Committee of the Red Cross, League of Red Cross Societies
1962	Linus Pauling
1961	Dag Hammarskjöld
1960	Albert Lutuli
1959	Philip Noel-Baker
1958	Georges Pire
1957	Lester Bowles Pearson
1956	No prize awarded
1955	No prize awarded
1954	Office of the United Nations High Commissioner for Refugees
1953	George C. Marshall

---

9 Joint founders of the Northern Ireland Peace Movement.

1952	Albert Schweitzer
1951	Léon Jouhaux
1950	Ralph Bunche
1949	Lord Boyd Orr
1948	No prize awarded
1947	Friends Service Council, American Friends Service Committee
1946	John R. Mott, Emily Greene Balch[10]
1945	Cordell Hull
1944	International Committee of the Red Cross
1943	No prize awarded
1942	No prize awarded
1941	No prize awarded
1940	No prize awarded
1939	No prize awarded
1938	Nansen International Office for Refugees
1937	Robert Cecil
1936	Carlos Saavedra Lamas
1935	Carl von Ossietzky
1934	Arthur Henderson
1933	Sir Norman Angell
1932	No prize awarded
1931	Jane Addams[11], Nicholas Murray Butler
1930	Nathan Söderblom
1929	Frank B. Kellogg
1928	No prize awarded

---

10 Won for her work with the Women's International League for Peace and Freedom, which she helped found.

11 Founder of the first settlement houses in the U.S.A. and president of the Women's International League for Peace and Freedom.

1927	Ferdinand Buisson, Ludwig Quidde
1926	Aristide Briand, Gustav Stresemann
1925	Sir Austen Chamberlain, Charles G. Dawes
1924	No prize awarded
1923	No prize awarded
1922	Fridtjof Nansen
1921	Hjalmar Branting, Christian Lange
1920	Léon Bourgeois
1919	Woodrow Wilson
1918	No prize awarded
1917	International Committee of the Red Cross
1916	No prize awarded
1915	No prize awarded
1914	No prize awarded
1913	Henri La Fontaine
1912	Elihu Root
1911	Tobias Asser, Alfred Fried
1910	Permanent International Peace Bureau
1909	Auguste Beernaert, Paul Henri d'Estournelles de Constant
1908	Klas Pontus Arnoldson, Fredrik Bajer
1907	Ernesto Teodoro Moneta, Louis Renault
1906	Theodore Roosevelt
1905	Bertha von Suttner[12] ♀
1904	Institute of International Law
1903	Randal Cremer
1902	Élie Ducommun, Albert Gobat
1901	Henry Dunant, Frédéric Passy

---

12 A radical pacifist and novelist from Austria. The first woman to win the award.

Of the 33 women and 733 men who have won a Nobel Prize, the only ones to have been awarded it in two different categories are Marie Curie (Physics in 1903 and Chemistry in 1911) and Linus Carl Pauling (Chemistry in 1954 and Peace in 1962). This is not the only reason that Marie Curie (1867–1934) is to be forever worshipped and adored. See also page 22.

Placing a Bet at the Horse Races

One night in 1783, the following bet was placed at Brooks's gentlemen's club on St. James's Street in London: "Ld. Cholmondley has given two guineas to Ld. Derby, to receive 500 Gs. whenever his Lordship fucks a woman in a Balloon one thousand yards from the surface of the earth." Since then, sadly, betting has become somewhat more tame in its focus.

The most common setting for betting these days is the horse races. This outdoor equestrian event is riddled with peril—one need only consult *My Fair Lady* (1964) or *Pretty Woman* (1990) to confirm this. Inappropriate attire, unseemly shouting, and drinking too much in the clubhouse are just a few of the potential sources of humiliation. Placing a bet, however, need not be one of them.

PLACES TO BET

- **The betting stations.** Also known as "windows," these are found at the race ground itself. All bets are pooled and then used to pay the winnings, with the result that the odds on a horse may well change between placing the bet and the start of the race. It also means that the house is guaranteed to make money on every race. This kind of wagering system is known as "pari-mutuel" (from the French term *pari mutuel*, meaning "mutual betting"), and is common in horse racing, greyhound racing, and a ball game called jai-alai that is particularly popular in southern Florida.

- **Off-track betting.** Such establishments are colloquially referred to as "O.T.B.'s" and are found in cities across the country. Full of cigarette smoke, detritus, and depressed-looking men. Best avoided.

- **Online.** The only option for which pajamas are acceptable attire.

ODDS

If one's horse should triumph, winnings are calculated on the basis of the horse's odds (also known as "price"). If the odds are long (e.g., 50/1), the horse is unlikely to win; if they are short, e.g., 2/1, the horse stands a good chance of winning but, of course, one will win less if it does. Odds can be given in one of three ways:

- **Even money (or "evens").** This is when the bookmaker offers a return that is double the amount staked on a win bet—often displayed as 1/1. So if one's stake is $10, the win will be $20.

- **Odds against.** This is when the bookmaker offers a return that is more than double the amount staked for a win, i.e., if one's stake is $10, a winning bet at 2/1 (pronounced "two to one" or "two to one *against*") will return $20 plus the original stake of $10, making a total of $30.

- **Odds on.** This is when the bookmaker offers a return that is less than double the amount staked for a win bet, with the word "on" indicating that the odds are reversed. A successful $10 bet at 1/2 (pronounced "two to one *on*"), will return just $5 plus your stake, making a total of $15.

TYPES OF BETS

The types of bets one can place are numerous and can be dizzyingly complicated. Some of the more common types include:

- **Win.** One's horse must finish first. The most straightforward and best choice for the beginner.

- **Place.** One's horse must finish first or second. A more flexible option, but one with lower returns.

- **Show.** One's horse must finish first, second, or third.

- **Accumulator.** A bet involving more than one horse with the winnings from each selection going onto the next.

- **Exacta.** One must pick the two horses that will finish first and second in exact order.

- **Trifecta.** One must pick the three horses that will finish first, second, and third in exact order.

- **Superfecta.** One must pick the four horses that will finish first, second, third, and fourth in exact order. Only for the very lucky or reckless.

PICKING A HORSE

The simplest way to study a horse's past form is to purchase a "race card" on arrival at the racecourse—this is not in fact a card, but a booklet that provides basic details on all the day's runners and riders. Factors to consider include: has the horse won before on a similar distance? Under what conditions has it performed best? What is the going (i.e., the quality of the ground) like today? What kind of going does the horse prefer? Hard? Soft? Is the horse carrying significantly more or less weight than in previous races? Who is the jockey? Who is the trainer? Alternatively, one can simply choose a horse with an auspicious-sounding name— the same name as one's pet rabbit or first boyfriend, perhaps. If still undecided, one should make one's way to the parade ring, where the horses are walked out before each race. This is an excellent opportunity to assess their fitness up close. At the same time, one may also consider extra factors such as the jockeys' outfits (known as "silks")—since as any woman knows, a pleasing color scheme is of paramount importance to becoming a winner.

Once all these important decisions have been made, the money for the bet is handed over and one is given a ticket which must be produced in order to collect any winnings. Bets can be made until moments before the race commences. Though impossible to explain in scientific terms, experience proves that the louder one cheers for one's horse, the more chance it has of winning. One final point: it is advisable to stay sober throughout. This, however, tends to prove trickier than it sounds.

What to Cook for a "Wild" Dinner Party

In 1940, *They Can't Ration These* by the Vicomte de Mauduit was published in response to the outbreak of war. A French aristocrat living in England, the Vicomte sought to reveal the pleasures of living off the nation's natural resources—its fields, woods, seashores, and suchlike. These same resources may also be found in the United States. The recipes he proposes have the additional advantage that most of the ingredients are essentially free.

NETTLE SOUP

Pick, wash, and dry a pint glass worth of nettles. Scatter them into a saucepan containing a pint of water, then add some salt. Stir vigorously, then simmer for ten minutes. In a separate pan, melt an ounce of bacon fat, then add an ounce of flour, then the nettles and water. Cook slowly for another five minutes, stirring all the time. Add a smidgen of hot milk, then a few croutons, and serve.

ROAST HEDGEHOG

Preparing the hedgehog is the mildly tricky bit. First, clean out the hedgehog's insides. Then roll it in some moist clay until it is generously coated, and bake it in a moderately hot oven until the clay is dry and hard. Use a hammer to shatter the clay; when it comes off, the prickles and top skin of the hedgehog will stick to it. Finally, skin the legs. Then simply roast the remaining animal as you might a chicken, and serve.

SOME OTHER WILD FOODS TO LOOK OUT FOR NEXT TIME THERE IS A DINNER PARTY TO PLAN

samphire · starling · eel

blackberries · dandelions · squirrel

What to Cook for a Slightly Less "Wild" Dinner Party

A roast chicken is the perfect choice for any dinner party. It is incredibly easy to make, yet always looks terribly impressive, humans being the very visual creatures they are. Simply place the chicken in a roasting tray and smear it with butter, garlic, lemon (the juice, squeezed, and the rind, grated), and thyme—on its skin, up its bottom, wherever. The more the merrier, especially with the butter. Cook in an oven preheated to 400° F for about forty-five minutes for every couple of pounds of chicken, plus an extra twenty minutes for luck, basting it occasionally.

It is a truth universally acknowledged that one can never

make too many roast potatoes. Boil the potatoes for five to ten minutes, then drain them in a colander, shaking the colander vigorously in order to roughen up the outsides. Add the potatoes to the roasting tray with the chicken and cook for about an hour, turning once, until crispy.

Finally, liven the whole meal up with unusual or exotic vegetables such as red cabbage (the day before, ideally, fry an onion; then add a chopped red cabbage, a chopped cooking apple, two or three tablespoons of brown sugar, and a liberal amount of cider vinegar; then simmer for a couple of hours) or sweet potatoes (roast them just like a potato but without the preboiling—sweet potatoes are less dense than normal potatoes, hence they cook more quickly).

For dessert, see page 91.

A Selection of the World's Largest Cut Diamonds

GOLDEN JUBILEE

Size	Shape	Color	Collection
545.67 carats[1]		Yellowish-brown	Thai crown jewels

History
Discovered in 1985 in De Beers's Premier mine in South Africa and presented to the King of Thailand, King Rama IX, in 1997, on the fiftieth anniversary of his coronation.

---

1 The carat derives its name from the seeds of a carob tree, which in Asia were once used to balance scales. Each seed uniformly weighed 200 milligrams and became the standard for measuring the weight of diamonds. So to convert a carat weight into grams, simply divide it by five—so, for example, the Golden Jubilee at 545.67 weighs about 109 grams.

CULLINAN I (also known as the Great Star of Africa)

Size	Shape	Color	Collection
530.20 carats		Colorless	British crown jewels

History
The Cullinan was originally the largest diamond ever found—3106.75 carats. It was mined in South Africa in 1905 and named after the owner of the mine, Sir Thomas Cullinan. It was later cut into a number of smaller pieces. Cullinan I is now estimated to be worth about $380 million.

INCOMPARABLE

Size	Shape	Color	Collection
407.48 carats		Yellow	Diamond dealer in the U.S.

History
Discovered in central Africa in the 1980s.

CULLINAN II (also known as the Lesser Star of Africa)

Size	Shape	Color	Collection
317.40 carats		Colorless	British crown jewels

History
See Cullinan I, above.

Great Mogul

Size	Shape	Color	Collection
280.00 carats		Colorless	Unknown

History
Discovered in India in 1650. Named after Shah Jehan, who built the Taj Mahal.

Nizam

Size	Shape	Color	Collection
277.00 carats		Colorless	Private collection in the U.S.

History
Also discovered in India, from the 1830s the Nizam was owned by the Nizam (i.e., the ruler) of Hyderabad.

Centenary

Size	Shape	Color	Collection
273.85 carats		Colorless	British crown jewels

History
The world's largest flawless diamond, found in South Africa in the same mine as the Cullinan I.

GREAT TABLE

Size	Shape	Color	Collection
250.00 carats		Pink	Unknown

History

Recorded in Golconda in south-central India in 1642; thereafter, it disappeared. The rumor is that it was recut and is now part of the crown jewels of Iran.

JUBILEE

Size	Shape	Color	Collection
245.35 carats		Colorless	Private collection in France

History

Mined in South Africa in 1895, in its rough form it weighed almost 651 carats; however, it was cut into its current form two years later, which was also the year of Queen Victoria's Diamond Jubilee, hence the name.

DE BEERS

Size	Shape	Color	Collection
234.50 carats		Yellow	Private collection in India

History

The first major discovery of the De Beers Corporation came fom the Kimberley mine in South Africa.

RED CROSS

Size	Shape	Color	Collection
205.00 carats		Yellow	Unknown

History

Put up for sale at Christie's in 1918, the British newspaper the Times *described it as follows: "Large and square-shaped, it has been cut with many facets and is of that pale canary yellow color which is so sought after by Indian Princes. The play of the stone is very vivid. In artificial light it is much more luminous than a white stone. After exposure to brilliant light it emits the rays it has absorbed, and thus becomes self-luminous in the dark. Another rare feature is that a Maltese Cross is distinctly visible in the top facet. Hence the double appropriateness of its name, the Red Cross Diamond."*

For further information on diamonds, refer to Marilyn Monroe's stance on the matter, expressed in the song "Diamonds Are a Girl's Best Friend" from the seminal and brilliant film *Gentlemen Prefer Blondes* (1953)[1]:

> The French were bred to die for love.
> They delight in fighting duels.
> But I prefer a man who lives,
> And gives expensive jewels.
> A kiss on the hand may be quite continental,
> But diamonds are a girl's best friend.
> A kiss may be grand, but it won't pay the rental
> On your humble flat, or help you at the automat.
> Men grow cold as girls grow old,
> And we all lose our charms in the end.
> But square-cut or pear-shaped,

---

1 Based on the equally seminal and brilliant book *Gentlemen Prefer Blondes* (1925) by Anita Loos, a feminist text well ahead of its time. The film version, though, simply features lots of fancy frocks and a scene with Jane Russell in a gym surrounded by topless bodybuilders.

These rocks don't lose their shape.
Diamonds are a girl's best friend.
Tiffany's! Cartier! Black Star, Frost, Gorham!
Talk to me, Harry Winston, tell me all about it!
There may come a time when a lass needs a lawyer,
But diamonds are a girl's best friend.
There may come a time when a hard-boiled employer
Thinks you're awful nice.
But get that ice or else no dice.
He's your guy when stocks are high,
But beware when they start to descend.
It's then that those louses go back to their spouses.
Diamonds are a girl's best friend.
I've heard of affairs that are strictly platonic,
But diamonds are a girl's best friend.
And I think affairs that you must keep liaisonic
Are better bets if little pets get big baguettes.
Time rolls on and youth is gone,
And you can't straighten up when you bend.
But stiff back or stiff knees,
You stand straight at Tiffany's.
Diamonds!
Diamonds!
I don't mean rhinestones.
But Diamonds
Are a Girl's Best Friend!

(Music by Jules Styne, lyrics by Leo Robin)

Homeopathy

There are an awful lot of people who are unaware of the wonders of homeopathy solely because of the persistent and absurd war between "conventional" and "unconventional" medicine. Homeopathy is a complementary medicine in every sense of the word. No respectable homeopath would eschew antibiotics if someone had pneumonia or deny someone a local anesthetic if they were having a tooth out. Instead, they would prescribe an immune-boosting remedy to work together with the antibiotic or offer a homeopathic gel to apply to the gum after the tooth is removed. People who use homeopathy have a tendency to be somewhat smug about it, due to the fact that they usually get better more quickly than those who deny themselves this extra help.

Homeopathic remedies most commonly come in the form of tiny white pills that taste slightly sweetish. One puts a pill in one's mouth, ideally straight from the container so that it does not react unduly with chemicals or germs on one's fingers. Try to keep the pill in the mouth for as long as possible while it dissolves— do not chew or swallow it. Caffeine and alcohol should be avoided while taking such remedies.

In a perfect world, we would all have our own homeopathic doctor who understands our constitution and prescribes remedies specifically for us. But failing this, buy a book and go for trial and error. It is often difficult to reach a definitive conclusion: for instance, if someone is bruised in an accident and is given Arnica (one every half an hour for two or three hours and then a couple a day), they would eventually get better anyway, wouldn't they? Or, if someone feels sick and is given Nux vom, the nausea might have disappeared regardless. This lack of proof means that some people discount homeopathy entirely; those who use it, however, know that it works. Though it might be all in the mind, of course. . . .

TEN HOMEOPATHIC REMEDIES TO TRY

• If one is bruised, either mentally or physically, take Arnica. This is the most amazing remedy, useful for any kind of physical exhaustion, accident, dental work, operation, and even emotional trauma.

• For nausea or an upset tummy, take Nux vom.

• For cuts or sores, take Hypericum.

• For a cut that might get infected, use Calendula—it is the homeopathic antiseptic.

• If one feels the onset of flu, take Gelsemium or, even better, a little vial of a cocktail of homeopathic remedies called Oscillococcinum. It purportedly zaps the flu before it has time to take over.

• For the first stages of a cold, take Aconite.

• For a cough, take Drosera.

• For muscle aches, take Rhus tox.

• For period pains, take magnesium phosphate.

• For a headache, take Byronia.

Therapy

Contrary to popular belief, therapy does actually work—it is not just for psychopaths. If it is considered reasonable to pay someone to clean your house, then why not your head? The key is simply not to do it forever. There are many different types of therapy, all of which can, in essence, be traced back to the work of Sigmund Freud (1856–1939).

TYPES OF THERAPY

Psychodynamic

By 1896, Freud had developed a method of working with neurotic Victorian women that he called "psychoanalysis." It involved making them lie on a couch and talk to him about what was going on in their overemotional heads. His approach focused on the dynamics of the relationship between the psyche and the external world. The resulting "psychodynamic" therapies concentrate on the feelings (often unconscious, according to Freud) we have about ourselves or other people.

Psychodynamic treatment involves harping on about past experiences, endlessly surmising how these may have led to one's present situation, and why The Past may now be ruining one's life. The therapist tends to say little, other than to make various opaque "interpretations" of the client's statements. Any understanding gained from psychodynamic discussion allegedly frees the client from the future repetition of destructive patterns. If one's problems are long-standing, treatment may last a good many expensive months, even years. Woody Allen, after spending forty years on the couch, eventually admitted that he thought the process irrelevant—despite once consulting his shrink on the decision to make the switch from polyester sheets to cotton ones.

Humanistic

In the 1940s and 1950s, American psychologist Carl Rogers developed his own ideas in response to Freud's psychodynamic ones. Now known as "humanistic" therapy, Rogers's "nice" therapy places significant emphasis on recognizing human capabilities in areas such as personal choice, creativity, and development (thus making it more of an artistic, rather than scientific, approach). It also focuses on the therapist holding "unconditional positive regard" for the client—in other words, the client is always right and the therapist's opinion is of no importance. Hence, this "client-centered" humanistic therapy can easily let one off the hook, with the therapist saying things like "I can see that makes you feel sad" a lot, and always taking the client's side.

However, from the 1960s onward the humanistic movement branched out into increasingly "relationship-centered" types of therapy—among them Gestalt, Existential and Transactional Analysis. These focus on a more equal relationship between the client and the therapist in which the therapist gives (often highly challenging) feedback in order to help individuals recognize their own strengths.

Behavioral

Modern behavioral therapy first emerged in the 1950s and evolved under the influence of theories of how people learn. Rejecting the notion of "hidden" aspects of the mind, which cannot be proven to exist, practitioners in the behavioral tradition began to focus on what could actually be observed in the outside world. Behavioral methods attempt to change patterns of behavior more directly. These methods can be fairly brutal: patients are often forced to overcome their fears by spending increasing amounts of time in the situation they dread or being made to endure various anxiety-provoking experiences. Patients are given "homework" and have to keep diaries and practice new skills between sessions.

Behavioral therapies are thought to be effective for all manner of issues, ranging from anxiety to obsessive-compulsive disorders to sexual difficulties. Relief from symptoms often occurs quite quickly, which is why this approach is seen as a bargain, compared to the financial drain of the other, talking cures.

Cognitive Behavioral Therapy, however, combines both. Rather than focusing on the past, it aims at changing thinking patterns directly and encourages discussion to help rid oneself of silly thinking. It is currently being lauded as *the* new cure for depression.

Family/Marital

There comes a time in everyone's life when one finally has to realize that not *all* of one's problems can be blamed on other people—husbands, mothers, or more popular siblings, for example. To this end, family or marital therapy, which began in the 1960s and was born of a technical and philosophical departure from traditional individual treatment, advocates everyone sitting down—together—to have a good chat. Squirming, all the participants put their side across. The therapist then attempts to dodge the flying furniture and focus objectively on what is really going on.

A doctor can make referrals to a qualified psycho-therapist; otherwise, word of mouth is the best recommendation, so be brave and ask around. The therapist must have a *recognized* (and not just by themselves) qualification. Do not be afraid to shop about for someone who suits: one would not dream of buying the first winter coat one tried on, after all.

The Thank-You Letter

WHEN TO WRITE A THANK-YOU LETTER

Always.

(For the single exception to this rule, see page 32 on Group Sex).

The concept of a thank-you letter is actually a misnomer. A letter suggests someone with too much time on her hands—unless, obviously, it is in response to an amazingly spectacular present or an entire week's hospitality. In almost all other cases, a simple postcard will suffice. Make a point of picking up suitable postcards wherever you go—it is eminently satisfying to be able to match the postcard to the recipient in a witty or wise way. For inspiration for the composition of such missives, refer to the two examples below: one from Samuel Johnson thanking Lord Bute for a royal pension, which is rather courtly and conventional in style, followed by one from Lord Byron to his publisher John Murray that is very dismissive of a present of books, but so well written that it all but makes up for the insult.

July 20, 1762.

> *My Lord,*
>
> *When the bills were yesterday delivered to me by Mr Wedderburne, I was informed by him of the future favours which his Majesty has by your Lordship's recommendation been induced to intend for me.*
>
> *Bounty always receives part of its value from the manner in which it is bestowed; your Lordship's kindness includes every circumstance that can gratify delicacy, or enforce obligation. You have conferred your favours on a Man who has neither alliance nor interest, who has nor merited them by services, nor courted them by officiousness; you have spared him the shame of solicitation, and the anxiety of suspense. What has been thus elegantly given, will, I hope, not*

be reproachfully enjoyed; I shall endeavour to give
your Lordship the only recompense, which generosity
desires, the gratification of finding that your benefits
are not improperly bestowed. I am, My Lord,
Your Lordship's most obliged,
Most obedient, and most humble servant,
Sam. Johnson

September 12, 1821.
Dear Sir,
. . . I have no patience with the sort of trash you send me
out by way of books; except Scott's novels, and three or four
other things, I never saw such work or works. Campbell
is lecturing—Moore idling—Southey twaddling—
Wordsworth driveling—Coleridge muddling—Joanna
Baillie piddling—Bowles quibbling, squabbling, and
sniveling. . . .

Yours,
Byron.

~~How to~~ Make an Abode Gemütlich in Just Three-quarters of an Hour (or, "A Daffodil in a Glass Jar")

The concept of "a daffodil in a glass jar" is that literally
any home, temporary or otherwise, can be dramatically
improved simply by doing a few small things to make
it cozy. This is regardless of whether the dwelling is
a postcollege starter apartment, a family vacation *gîte*
in France or a corporate rental in Los Angeles: the
principle is the same.

First, tidy up, throw away ruthlessly, and put a daffodil in a (very clean) glass jar (or, failing that, a wine bottle) with water in it on the table.

Next, arrange the books on the bookcase so they are not too neat (they need to look used) but are vaguely ordered. Buy some ticking fabric and cut it up to make a tablecloth, a throw or some curtains (even if they are nailed up and then tied back with a ribbon). Track down a blanket or rug and put it on the chair or sofa. Tidy the kitchen, then put out a fresh loaf of bread on a bread board with a bread knife and some fresh coffee in a tin (for the smell alone, even if one does not use it). If possible, have bare boards instead of carpet or linoleum (if the boards cannot be stripped or polished, they can at least be painted gray or pale blue—although this might be pushing it in three-quarters of an hour; see below). Have a pile of newspapers, books, knitting, sewing, anything to make the room look lived in. If there is no furniture, use wooden champagne boxes for anything from a low chair to a side table to a bookshelf. If unable or not allowed to get rid of depressing furniture, cover it with the mattress-ticking; and try to acquire one or two old things—a wooden box, a blue-and-white plate, a clock, a bentwood chair—as these will improve over time, whereas the cheap, modern stuff will deteriorate into junk. To this end, it is far better to buy something old at an auction than to buy something new that will look outdated all too soon.

Above all, aim for simplicity: the chic-est rooms are those that have the confidence not to look as though anyone has tried too hard. And for those who have more than three-quarters of an hour, the next most transforming thing is paint.

Rain

1. a. The condensed vapor of the atmosphere, falling in drops large enough to attain a sensible velocity; the fall of such drops.

c. 825 Vesp. Psalter *cxlvi. 8 Se oferwiro heofen mid wolcnum & gearwao eoroan regn.* a *1000 ÆLFRIC* Gen. *vii. 4 Ic . . . sende ren . . . ofer eoroan. 1154* O.E. Chron. *(Laud MS.) an. 1117 Mid punre & lihtinge & reine & hagole.* a *1200 ORMIN 8622 Wel hallf feorpe eer . . . comm na reeen onn eorpe. c 1250* Gen. & Ex. *3265 Dhunder, and leuene, and rein oor-mong God sent. c 1330 R. BRUNNE* Chron. Wace *(Rolls) 6827 be arewes come so pykke so reyn. c 1386 CHAUCER* Monk's T. *183 In reyn with wilde beestes walked hee.* —— Prioress' T. *222 Hise salte teeris trickled doun as reyn. c 1449 PECOCK* Repr. *II. Ii. 146 To couere him fro reyne and fro other sturne wedris. 1535 STEWART* Cron. Scot. *III. 257 Fers as ane eill war new tane in the rane. 1635 SWAN* Spec. M. *iv. § 2 (1643) 58 The rain, proceeding from those vapours which we call the clouds. 1710 ADDISON* Tatler *No. 218 ¶ 2 A black Cloud falling to the Earth in long Trails of Rain. 1752 HUME* Ess. & Treat. *(1777) II. 90 There is a certain uniformity in the operation of the sun, rain, and earth. SCOTT* Lady of L. *v. xv, Fierce Roderick . . . shower'd his blows like wintry rain. 1878 HUXLEY* Physiogr. *41 We may fairly expect the formation of rain to be preceded by that of cloud.*

—Edited from the entry on "Rain" in the *Oxford English Dictionary*

"Rainy today, isn't it?" This is surely one of the most commonly heard conversation-openers in America, so one might as well have something interesting to say in response. Although "Did you know that the most rainfall ever to fall in a single day was on July 25, 1979 in Alvin, Texas?" is perhaps not a reply that will ensure the admiring glances of all within earshot, it may at least raise the tone of the conversation up a notch from "Mmmm, isn't it?"

How rain happens

Water evaporates into the air from oceans, seas, rivers, and lakes, and also from plants, as well as in smallish amounts from volcanic gases belowground and from burning fossil fuels aboveground. As the water rises upward, it cools, condensing from a gas to a liquid to form droplets. These droplets then condense around miniscule dust particles; the result is a cloud. Each of the droplets continues to increase in size as new droplets in turn condense onto them. The more this happens, the heavier each droplet becomes, until it is heavy enough to fall from the bottom of the cloud.

However, if the cloud is high, the air dry and warm, or the droplet still small enough that it falls relatively slowly, there is a good chance that it will evaporate entirely before it reaches the ground. Alternatively, it might be caught by an upward draft of air. In this case, the cycle begins again, the droplets remaining suspended in the atmosphere. The more this happens, the bigger each droplet becomes, which is how really fierce storms are created.

Eventually, the droplet becomes so heavy that gravity takes over, regardless of any upward drafts of air. Even on the way down, it might continue to increase in size as other droplets collide and then coalesce with it. The result is that, one way or another, it reaches the ground.

Also note that, technically, rain is only rain when the droplets are more than 0.02 inches (0.5 mm) in diameter. Any smaller and they are classified as drizzle.

In the future, significant changes in rainfall patterns are expected, as winters get wetter (and summers get drier). One may as well get used to it—though clearly this is easier said than done when waiting for the bus in one's new suede boots in the midst of a thunderstorm. Be inspired by John Updike's spin on the matter: "Rain is grace; rain is the sky condescending to the earth; without rain, there would be no life."

Those who really hate the rain should move to Florida, which in 2006 was the driest state in the country with only three inches of rainfall all year. Alternatively, splash out on a Marc Jacobs umbrella, which are among the most fabulous available—they *never* get left on the bus. Trivial as it might appear, an umbrella one adores really can contribute quite considerably to one's everyday level of happiness. For it means that when looking out of the window of a morning, only to see that it is raining *again*, one's reaction shifts from "Drat, when will it end?" to "Whoopee, a reason to use my umbrella"—which, on a day-to-day basis, genuinely does make all the difference.

A SELECTION OF SONGS TO SING IN THE RAIN

"Singing in the Rain" —*Gene Kelly*

"Raindrops Keep Falling on My Head"
—*Burt Bacharach*

"Rainy Days and Mondays" —*The Carpenters*

"Purple Rain" —*Prince*

"Why Does It Always Rain on Me?" —*Travis*

"Don't Rain on My Parade" —*Barbra Streisand*

"November Rain" —*Guns 'n' Roses*

"It's Raining Men" —*The Weather Girls*

"Raining in My Heart" —*Buddy Holly*

"Here Comes the Rain Again" —*The Eurythmics*

"A Hard Rain's Gonna Fall" —*Bob Dylan*[1]

"Another Fucking Song About the Rain"
—*Daniel Johnston & Jack Medicine*

Diets

The first truly popular fad diet was invented in the nineteenth century by William Banting, a rotund British casket maker who, at an advanced stage in life, was appalled to discover that he was no longer able to reach down to tie his own shoelaces, such was his girth. His doctor advised him to give up his usual intake of bread, butter, milk, sugar, beer, and potatoes, owing to the fact they contained too much "starch and saccharine matter, tending to create fat, and should be avoided altogether." Banting followed this advice

---

[1] Some might prefer the Roxy Music version.

and made some radical changes to his eating regime, changes later detailed in his *Letter on Corpulence*. First published in 1863, it quickly became America's first best-selling low-carb diet book.

AN EXTRACT FROM *LETTER ON CORPULENCE* BY WILLIAM BANTING (1863)

For breakfast, at 9.0 A.M., I take five to six ounces of either beef, mutton, kidneys, broiled fish, bacon, or cold meat of any kind except pork or veal; a large cup of tea or coffee (without milk or sugar), a little biscuit, or one ounce of dry toast; making together six ounces solid, nine liquid.

For dinner, at 2.0 P.M., Five or six ounces of any fish except salmon, herrings, or eels, any meat except pork or veal, any vegetable except potato, parsnip, beetroot, turnip, or carrot, one ounce of dry toast, fruit out of a pudding not sweetened, any kind of poultry or game, and two or three glasses of good claret, sherry, or Madeira—champagne, port, and beer forbidden; making together ten to twelve ounces solid, and ten liquid.

For tea, at 6.0 P.M. Two or three ounces of cooked fruit, a rusk or two, and a cup of tea without milk or sugar; making two to four ounces solid, nine liquid.

For supper, at 9.0 P.M. Three or four ounces of meat or fish, similar to dinner, with a glass or two of claret or sherry and water; making four ounces solid and seven liquid.

For nightcap, if required, A tumbler of grog (gin, whisky, or brandy, without sugar) or a glass or two of claret or sherry.

THE WORLD'S WORST DIETS

ATKINS DIET

Date invented	Inventor	Textbook
1972	Robert C. Atkins	*Dr. Atkins' Diet Revolution* (1972); *Dr. Atkins' New Diet Revolution* (1992)

Description:
The ultimate modern low-carb, high-protein diet. Any diet that drives its devotees to carry slices of ham and cheese around in their jacket pockets, while at the same time forbidding them to eat carrots or beetroot, is clearly a preposterous one. Despite this, even perfectly intelligent people have been known to give it a go. This is because it does work—but only in the short term, and with side effects including body odor and heart problems.

SLIMFAST

Date invented	Inventor	Textbook
1977	S. Daniel Abraham	www.slimfast.com

Description:
A Slim-Fast milkshake for breakfast and lunch, followed by a "normal" supper. Fine for those happy to subsist primarily on milkshakes, but otherwise . . .

GRAPEFRUIT DIET

Date invented	Inventor	Textbook
		n/a
1930s	No single person or organization has claimed credit, though it was certainly popularized by a number of now-forgotten Hollywood starlets.	

Description
Eat half a grapefruit with every meal. Much more effective is half a pineapple, however. See below.

BEVERLY HILLS DIET

Date invented	Inventor	Textbook
1981	Julie Mazel	*The Beverly Hills Diet* (1981), followed by *The New Beverly Hills Diet* (1996), both by Judy Mazel

Description

Pineapple is to be eaten with every meal (interchanged occasionally with mango and papaya). This does actually work. Pineapple is Nature's only creation to contain an enzyme called bromelein, which basically digests protein—in other words, it eats away at fat. It is not a particularly healthy way to lose weight, however.

CABBAGE SOUP DIET

Date invented	Inventor	Textbook
Mid-1990s	Again, no single person or organization has claimed credit	n/a

Description

Eat as much cabbage soup as you like! Only for dimwits. Or for those who enjoy breaking wind.

THE WORLD'S BEST DIET

There is only one diet that actually works in the long term. It is this: Eat less unhealthy food, eat more healthy food, and exercise more often. It is not rocket science. When one wants to overindulge, fine, great, but overindulge on delicious ratatouille with brown rice, on juicy strawberries, or on sweet edamame. And do not do it every day. And do some exercise in between. Dull it may be, but it also, annoyingly, works.

How Humans Spread

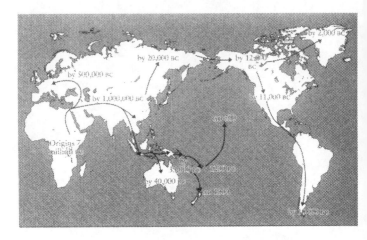

The Drinks Party

The drinks party is without a doubt the most challenging social battlefield of the new millennium. Whether it is birthday drinks at a local dive bar or the launch of a new range of jewel-encrusted men's underpants at the Ritz, the first few moments of these occasions tend to conform to few people's idea of a rollicking good time. Plunging headlong into a room full of acquaintances already all chit-chattering away at each other? Dancing around the difficulty of endless introductions? Eating standing up and with one hand? No thanks. But needs must, and as many of us become increasingly pressed for time, the drinks party has become the perfect way to squeeze numerous engagements into the same rainy Friday night. It is therefore important to find a way to negotiate them *with* charm and grace and *without* (too many) faux pas or (too much) falling over.

HOW TO CIRCULATE

Where the circumference of the circle is approximately equal to sixty minutes.

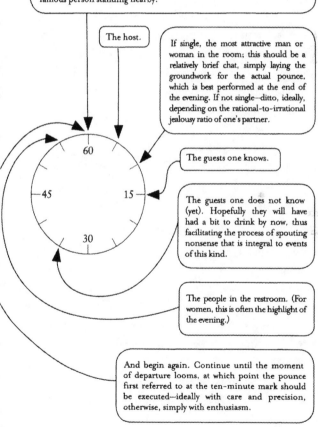

On arrival, tour the room. This is ostensibly an attempt to seek out the host or hostess, but is in actuality a form of reconnaissance. At certain parties, this activity is known as "doing a celebrity circuit," which, should the occasion arise, is something to get over and done with as soon as possible. As a tactic, it is hugely preferable to the alternative, which is spending the entire evening looking over the shoulder of the person one is pretending to converse with in order to catch a glimpse of a more famous person standing nearby.

The host.

If single, the most attractive man or woman in the room; this should be a relatively brief chat, simply laying the groundwork for the actual pounce, which is best performed at the end of the evening. If not single—ditto, ideally, depending on the rational-to-irrational jealousy ratio of one's partner.

The guests one knows.

The guests one does not know (yet). Hopefully they will have had a bit to drink by now, thus facilitating the process of spouting nonsense that is integral to events of this kind.

The people in the restroom. (For women, this is often the highlight of the evening.)

And begin again. Continue until the moment of departure looms, at which point the pounce first referred to at the ten-minute mark should be executed—ideally with care and precision, otherwise, simply with enthusiasm.

TEN COMMON "DRINKS PARTY" PITFALLS

1. Failure to introduce. If in doubt, err on the side of recklessness—it is hugely preferable to introduce people who, it turns out, have known each other since they were born on the same day, in the same hospital ward, than not to introduce them at all. The latter is a horrible rudeness that is swiftly becoming the bane of the modern drinks party.

2. Asking "So, what do you do for a living?" within the first fifteen minutes of a conversation with a new acquaintance. To ask too early places you in the camp of the judgmental or the lazy. Not to ask at all, however, is not without its own risks, for one might merrily chatter away to someone for an hour about the weather, only to find out later that they were actually conversing with Johnny Depp's personal dresser. So after an appropriate length of conversational time has passed, the most acceptable ploy is to find a way to bring the subject up naturally.

3. In an age where celebrity is all, it is not uncommon for the more cynical among us to be overly rude to this particular species, in a laudable attempt not to appear obsequious. The unfortunate result is that one ends up behaving in an even less friendly way than one would do to an unpleasant "civilian" (in the unmatchable terminology of Elizabeth Hurley). So do try to act normal. And should one be desperate to talk to the celebrity, do not line up with the hoi polloi. It is so undignified. Wait until

she or he is talking to just one other person, then approach. (At an office party, the same strategy applies for talking to the boss.)

4. Should a celebrity merely be the topic of conversation, rather than actually present, hazards remain. There are some celebrities about whom it is acceptable to talk at any kind of gathering. These include Jennifer Aniston, Tom Cruise, and Madonna—in other words, the A-list. The Pussycat Dolls are not such an inclusive subject, however. Celebrities also present an excellent recourse any time the conversation becomes too highbrow: there is little more fun to be had than asking the dean of Harvard what he thinks of the new Justin Timberlake album.

5. "Isn't it terrible what's happening in Chechnya?" "Did you enjoy the latest Dave Eggers?" Both of these are conversational salvos designed to strike fear into the heart of the aural recipient, but stay calm. Try not to repeat the gist of an opinion piece from the previous day's newspaper, an all-too-common ploy. Instead, the key is to hark back to the past when answering: the past never changes, whereas the present often does, which is why staying up-to-date can be tricky. An acceptable response to "Isn't it terrible what's happening in Chechnya?" might be something along the lines of "Well, it's always been a trouble spot, hasn't it? I mean, look at the 1830s: Ever since Nicholas I invaded, it's been part of Russia's plan to expand southward.

I think it's the mountains. . . ." Then gracefully steer the conversation back to safer territory: a recent mountain-climbing holiday, the melting of mountains around the world as result of global warming, or the many attractions of the Berkshires, for instance. Similarly, a pertinent response to "Did you enjoy the latest Dave Eggers?" might be "It was his previous book which really blew me away." An alternative approach, however, is simply to brazen it out: "I've never read any Dave Eggers. Explain to me what it is about him that gets people so excited." Remember, to be ignorant is fine, but to be fraudulent or pretentious is unforgivable.

6. It is unseemly to be seen stuffing one's face with food at a drinks party. This does not mean that food-stuffing cannot be done, however. One just has to employ a little stealth. During each conversation with someone new, limit oneself to eating just two of whatever delights are on offer. Then continue to circulate, and follow the same principle. *Et voilà*, a stomach full to bursting purely by dint of playing the social butterfly.

7. In *Modern Manners* (1992), Drusilla Beyfus comments on one particular conundrum of the drinks party: how to disengage. She writes, "No one is obliged to remain with the first people to whom they are introduced. A good moment for separation is when other people arrive to talk to someone else in the group. It would be oversensitive to feel miffed if people to whom you have been talking move on; it is quite in order for guests to wander off to pastures

new with some casual observation such as 'I must have a word with Matthew over there' or simply, 'I'm going to circulate.' It is not necessary to make any excuse, however." Yet in practice, this can be a difficult course to steer. It is only the brave, rude, or those with mild to severe Asperger's (which, to be fair, psychologists say is far more of us than one might think) who do not feel they ought to make some kind of attempt at an excuse. Everyone knows that it is an excuse, that one is not really going to get another drink, go to the bathroom, or ask someone in the far corner of the room a terribly important question—but accepted social mores mean that no one would ever have the bad taste to acknowledge this. An alternative approach, however, is to say something along the lines of "Right, I really ought to go and circulate I suppose, but may I take you with me?"—a simple but exceptionally charming way to disengage politely.

8. It is amazing how common it is to endure an entire drinks party without being asked a single question about oneself. Men of a certain type and age in particular tend to assume one has a boring job, especially if they know one is attending said party with a partner who has an interesting job: the logic goes that for there to be two interesting jobs in one relationship is simply impossible, since how would there be any time to do the laundry? The appropriate response is to refuse to be cowed. Instead, as soon as there is a pause in the conversation, launch (à propos of nothing) into "I was on *The Today Show* this morning" or "George Clooney made love to me at lunchtime" or

"I'm a professional hot-air ballooner, have you ever tried it?". If the topic is interesting enough, few will remember the somewhat abrupt manner in which it was first introduced. And if they do, then at least it will have brightened things up a little: be provocative, be surprising, but never, ever be dull.

9. When Virginia Woolf lamented that "Literature is strewn with the wreckage of men who have minded beyond reason the opinions of others," she could just as well have been talking about drinks parties. Nowhere else is the peculiarly human emotion known as embarrassment more frequently experienced. Some faux pas are avoidable: Never ask someone if they are going to so-and-so's party next week, never ask someone if they are pregnant, and never eat anything in public that resembles chocolate cake (it coats one's teeth so horribly easily). However, should an alternative metaphorical banana skin happen to present itself, remember that embarrassment is an emotion that is easily dealt with. The key is not to dwell on the hideous moment in question, but instead to pretend to oneself—vigorously, passionately, and with true commitment—that the faux pas simply never happened. Train the brain to believe this; insist to the brain that it must believe this. Yes, it is a form of delusional behavior; but a much underrated one, and one that really, truly works.

10. The trouble with drinks parties is that they instantly become less interesting, and less fun, the minute one is no longer on the lookout for sex.

For this, let us be honest, is the raison d'etre of most such gatherings. The only solution is to leave early; and in doing so, be comforted by the fact that it is always more dignified to leave before the sun sets on a party—in other words, while it is still at its zenith. And, finally, accept that the most interesting conversations always take place just as one is getting one's coat. This is a fact of life, and is to be embraced.

The Muses

In Greek mythology, the muses are the nine goddess daughters of Zeus, king of the gods, and Mnemosyne, the goddess of memory. They preside over the arts and sciences, ready and able at any moment to inspire artists, poets, philosophers, and musicians all around the world to produce great works. Some might call this a dull job; but to others, it represents the pinnacle of a lifetime's aspiration.

NAME	MUSE OF	EMBLEM *(a prop or pose used to distinguish one muse from another when depicting them in art, particularly Roman, Renaissance, and Neoclassical art)*
Calliope	Epic song	A writing tablet
Clio	History	A scroll and books
Erato	Love or erotic poetry	A lyre and a crown
Euterpe	Lyric song	A flute
Melpomene	Tragedy	A tragic mask

Name	Muse of	Emblem
Polyhymnia	Sacred song. Sometimes also geometry, mime, meditation, and agriculture.	A pensive expression
Terpsichore	Dance	Dancing and carrying a lyre
Thalia	Comedy	A comic mask
Urania	Astronomy	A staff and a celestial globe

How to Deliver a Baby

Ideally, go to a hospital and let them do it. However, in some situations this may prove impossible. If so, proceed as follows.

Lie the mother on the ground on top of the cleanest thing at hand—sheets ideally. Being on the ground also ensures that when the baby arrives, he or she does not slide or slip off anywhere. Put a pillow, makeshift or otherwise, under the mother's hips, as well as one under her back. Wash your hands as thoroughly as possible, after which you should avoid touching anything except for the mother, the baby, and the sheets. This is to prevent infection.

Next, peer between the mother's legs. As soon as the baby's head becomes visible, birth is imminent. There is a chance that the head will still be covered by the amniotic sac, a membrane-like substance—in which case, burst the membrane by pinching and then twisting it out of the way, thus releasing the amniotic fluid.

Everything will then start to speed up. Put your hand under the baby's head to guide it, making sure it does not shoot out too fast, but equally important, that it keeps on coming. As it comes out, it should naturally turn onto its side. If this is all happening, let nature take its course as much as possible.

Once the baby's head is out, wipe away fluid from the baby's mouth and nose to help it breathe. If the umbilical cord is wrapped around the baby's neck, try to slip it over the baby's head.

Guide, but do not pull, the shoulders out. The baby will then slide right out. Check the breathing, then wrap him or her up warmly, leaving the face uncovered.

Do not forget about the placenta, which appears ten to forty-five minutes afterward, and which also needs to be delivered.

How to Use a Compass

Travelers were once limited to using the position of the celestial bodies to guide them. Since then, methods have evolved to become somewhat less romantic, if more accurate. About a thousand years ago, the earliest recorded accounts of the use of a compass appeared in China, where it took the form of a magnetic needle floating in a bowl of water. In the modern age, we are blessed with printed maps, websites such as Streetmap or MapQuest, and global positioning systems. Nonetheless, an ability to use a compass remains a key survival skill for anyone considering setting forth into the jungle—concrete or otherwise.

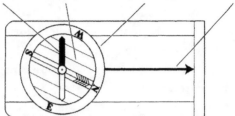

The most important thing to remember is that the red arrow inside a compass always points to magnetic north. Confusion can often arise from the idea that it will somehow be adjusted to point in the direction you wish to go. But it does not, it *only ever* points north, and you establish your route in relation to this.

If north is not the desired bearing, there are two ways of using a compass: either with a map, which will give a more accurate direction, or without a map, which is the most basic method and the one covered here.

Around the edge of the compass is a moveable ring marked with N, S, E, and W for north, south, east, and west. This is called the "compass housing." So to go southeast, for example, rotate the ring until the halfway point between S and E is aligned with the "direction of travel" arrow.

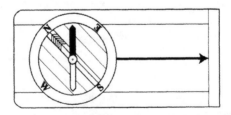

Hold the compass flat, then turn your body until the red compass needle is aligned with the parallel lines inside the compass housing. It is *extremely* important that the red end of the needle is pointing at the end marked N (rather than S)—otherwise you will set off 180 degrees in the wrong direction. Now walk in the direction of the "direction of travel" arrow, keeping the needle at all times within the parallel lines, and you will be walking southeast.

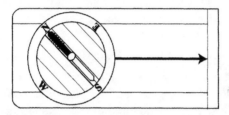

Then let the adventure begin. (See page 109 for the correct footwear to wear for the adventure in question.)

A Few World War II Heroines

ALA GERTNER (1912?–1945)

Ala Gertner was born in Bedzin in southern Poland into a wealthy Jewish family. In 1940 she was instructed to report to a nearby train station. She was transported to Geppersdorf, a Nazi labor camp, where she worked in the administrative office. A year later she was allowed home for a visit, but swiftly secured a posting at the local Judenrat (the Jewish civilian government), thus extending her leave indefinitely. Marriage to Bernard Holtz, who had worked at the desk next to hers in Geppersdorf, followed soon after.

About a month later Ala became one of the last

Jews in the area to be deported—this time, to Auschwitz. At the camp she worked in the warehouse, sorting the possessions of Jews who had been gassed; before long she was reassigned to the munitions factory. It was here that she became involved in a conspiracy to steal gunpowder out of the factory and smuggle it to the prisoners whose job it was to burn and bury corpses from the gas chambers. Their intention was to blow up one of the crematoriums, in turn sparking a camp uprising.

On October 7, 1944, one of the crematoriums was successfully detonated and several S.S. guards were shot. It was the only armed uprising ever to occur at Auschwitz.

It did not last long. Some of the men involved managed to escape after the uprising, but they were soon caught and shot. Ala and the other three women involved—Ester Wajcblum, Regina Safirsztajn, and Roza Robota—were accused of sabotage, resistance, and treason. On January 5, 1945, they were all hanged, just twenty-two days before the camp was liberated by the Red Army.

SOPHIE SCHOLL (1921–1943)

Sophie Scholl was the fourth of five children born into a middle-class, liberal, deeply Christian family. In 1942 she embarked upon a pursuit of degrees in philosophy and biology at Munich University. Her brother, Hans, was a student there at the same time, and it was through him that she met many of her friends. That summer she was obliged to enroll for war work at a metallurgical plant; around the same time, her father was sent to jail for making critical remarks about Hitler. These events galvanized her into joining the White Rose, a movement recently formed by Hans, which advocated passive resistance to the Nazis: "We want to try to show that everyone is in a position to contribute to the overthrow of the system. . . . It can be done only by the cooperation of many convinced, energetic people."[1] The White Rose's foremost tactic was to produce leaflets that criticized the Nazis and called for the restoration of a democratic government. These were distributed throughout central Germany, in particular to bar owners and university lecturers (both of whom were thought to be central to spreading the word).

On February 18, 1943, Sophie and Hans were distributing leaflets throughout their university building when they suddenly realized they were about to run out of time before classes finished for the day. Sophie raced upstairs to a third-floor landing and flung all of the remaining leaflets through the air into an inner courtyard below. She later attributed the decision to "either high spirits or stupidity." As students filed out of the lecture halls, the leaflets lay scattered all over the floor. Sophie and Hans were spotted by a local handyman who was also a member of the Nazi party, and who called the police.

Sophie explained her involvement in the White Rose thusly: "Somebody, after all, had to make a start. What we wrote and said is also believed by many others. They just do not dare express themselves as we did."[2] Just four days after their arrest, Sophie, Hans, and their friend Christoph Probst were condemned to death for treason. At five o'clock the same day, they were guillotined.

---

1 The White Rose. "Passive Resistance to National Socialism" (1943), Leaflet 3.

2 Sources: various.

VIRGINIA D'ALBERT-LAKE (1910–1997)

Virginia d'Albert-Lake was not only one of the few Americans to actively participate in the French Resistance during the war, she was also one of the very few female Americans to do so. Virginia was born in Dayton, Ohio, in 1910, but at the age of twenty-seven she married a Frenchman named Philippe d'Albert-Lake and moved to Paris. When the war broke out in 1939, her U.S. citizenship meant that she could easily have retreated home in search of safety; but she chose not to. Instead, she chose to stay and face the daily hardships brought on by Nazi occupation, just as her fellow Parisians were being forced to do. It was often the more trivial deprivations that proved the most annoying: "No more Glycerine—Tooth paste flows out of the tube!" reads an entry in Virginia's diary in March 1941.

From the fall of 1943 onward, Virginia and her husband were actively involved with the French Resistance. Their first contact with the movement came about when the local baker, Marcel Renard, asked them to come to dinner to act as interpreters for three American airmen he was sheltering in his house. Virginia and Philippe agreed, and, as Virginia recalled in her memoir, "We did not sleep much that night. Instead, we talked over the whole evening, discussed the boys and made a big decision: we would work in the Underground. Dangerous, yes, but we would be careful. It would be worth every risk run just to meet more boys like those tonight and lead them from right under the Germans' noses back home and the work yet to be accomplished."[3] In the course of the war, Virginia and Philippe helped a total of sixty-six downed airmen

3 Virginia d'Albert-Lake, *An American heroine in the French Resistance: the diary and memoir of Virginia d'Albert-Lake*, ed. Judy Barrett Litoff (2006), p. 93.

find their way back to Britain. As one of these men later described, "There we were, walking into this apartment after some pretty hairy experiences and being greeted by this beautiful woman who said, 'Hi fellas, how're you doing?' . . . She had no fear whatsoever."[4]

But in June 1944, as Victoria was bicycling through the French countryside with an airman she was escorting to a secret hideout, she was arrested by German police during a routine road check. Days of interrogation ensued, but at no point did she reveal to the Nazis the location of any of the hideouts, most notably one near Châteaudun that was of particular interest to her captors since by this time it sheltered more than one hundred and fifty Allied airmen.

In August 1944, Virginia was sent to Ravensbrück, a Nazi labor camp for women. It was an unimaginably horrific experience; when asked some years later how she coped, she replied, "It was a matter of morale. You couldn't let them see you weep. The women who wept at night usually were dead by the morning. You couldn't give in."[5] However, after six months there she was suddenly informed that she was to be transferred to a POW camp on the German-Swiss border, in large part due to the vigorous efforts of her mother in lobbying the American government.

When the war ended, the POW camp was liberated and Virginia was reunited with her family. As tales of her heroism spread, she received awards from the governments of the United States, Britain, Belgium, and France, including France's Legion of Honor, its highest honor for civilians. She remained in France with Philippe and her son, Patrick, until her death in 1997.

---

4 Ibid., p. xvii.

5 Ibid., p. xxxii.

VICTORIA SCHERAUTZ (1916–2006)[6]

Born into an aristocratic family in Warsaw, Victoria initially studied to be a painter. In 1938 she married a young politician, Alexander Scherautz, but when war broke out just a year later, they were both arrested by the Soviets. After three weeks aboard a cattle train, Victoria found herself under orders to start work on the construction of the Trans-Siberian railway—laying piece of track after piece of track in freezing temperatures in the depths of the Siberian forest. Before long she had the idea of using bricks made out of frozen mud to build makeshift huts. What resulted was a little village of huts for her and the other prisoners to take shelter in through the harsh winter. The response of the Soviet authorities, predictably enough, was to torture her, one result of which was that she was never able to have children.

In 1941 the Soviet Union was invaded by the Nazis, and Victoria was released, along with many of her fellow Polish prisoners. She escaped via train in the company of General Anders's expedition of seventy thousand Polish soldiers and civilians who were planning on marching into the Middle East, eventually to join the Allied forces in Italy. As the cattle train chugged out of the train station, scores of babies were thrown on board by women who were too weak to travel themselves, but who desperately wanted to give their children a chance of survival. Victoria caught one such baby just as his mother shouted over the noise of the engine, "His name is Yurek!"

---

6   Victoria's story only finally came to light with the publication in the *Guardian* (June 21, 2006) of an obituary written by her nephew.

Stopping off in India, Victoria established an orphanage for exiled Polish children. Her long-term aim, however, was to join the Polish army in Iran, where she hoped she might track down her husband, also an ex-POW. Embarking on this journey meant that she was forced to put Yurek up for adoption, and he was given to a wealthy Indian couple.

Victoria eventually made it to Iran, where she and Alexander were reunited. From then on, she worked for the Polish diplomatic missions and in organizing supplies for the British army in North Africa, until the war ended and the couple moved to London.

But while she was en route to attend General Anders's funeral in 1970, something extraordinary happened. On the plane, Victoria overheard a man in the seat behind her vividly describing to another passenger how, as a baby, a woman called Victoria had rescued him from a work camp in Siberia. From then on he had always considered her to be his mother; he even vaguely remembered her giving him up for adoption, an inevitably traumatic experience. He had ended up in England, having graduated from Edinburgh University and become a doctor. All that time, he had continued to hope he might one day be reunited with his mother. He still did.

Victoria, however, decided not to make herself known to Yurek. He was in his early thirties; he was accompanied by his pregnant wife; he had his whole life ahead of him, which she did not want to disrupt. She was simply relieved to know that he was alive and prospering. According to her nephew Wiktor Grodecki, she always said it was the happiest moment of her life.

VERE HODGSON (1901–1979)

Vere Hodgson may not have been a member of the Resistance or a prisoner in a labor camp, but she represents all those women who were left behind on the home front during the war and who attempted to continue to live "normal" lives. Just as brave in their own way as many of those who were on the front line, there was no way that the likes of Vere were going to let Hitler disrupt all that they knew and loved about the British way of life. Day-to-day, Vere helped run a charity in Notting Hill Gate. From June 1940 onward she also kept a diary, which was later published under the title *Few Eggs and No Oranges*. A vivid account of what it was like for women like her to live through the Blitz, the early pages in particular demonstrate that even in the midst of unimaginable awfulness, life goes on—it has to:[7]

> *November 7, 1940*
> *A terrible night! Guns never seemed to cease. Many bombs. No chance to go up the road. Slept at office until All Clear after 7 am. Not very refreshing to sleep in one's clothes, but the lovely bath helps a bit. Every district of London got it last night . . . Very difficult to get any eggs . . . almost impossible. Not a kipper to be had for a long time. Can't think what they have done with them . . . With regard to news on the Home Front, as if there was not enough to do, the Cat was taken ill! He was ailing before Xmas—could not jump on a chair. I fetched the vet. Between us we poured some liquid paraffin down his throat . . . I put the little animal up on a shelf near some warm pipes. He seems better.*

---

7   Vere Hodgson, *Few Eggs and No Oranges* (1999), p. 82 & p. 119.

January 31, 1941

Yesterday there was much going on above us and gunfire. Mrs. Starmer came back full of news of incendiaries in the City at Moorgate. The people rose out of the ground in droves to put them out! Everybody was laughing at the fun. She said it was like a football match and all enjoyed themselves.

A lady in the Mercury Cafe told me she was having lunch in Oxford Street. Suddenly a terrific wonk shook the place; all the cups and saucers danced and rattled about on the table. The man opposite her said calmly: "That was a bomb, wasn't it?" She replied: "I'm sure it was." And they continued to eat their meal.

Long~Term Investing

There is no doubt that the concept of investing is, to most of us, too dull even to contemplate before the age of about a hundred and six. But if one takes a moment to make a few calculations about how much money one could actually accumulate without too much trouble, it suddenly becomes a whole lot more interesting—a whole lot more, in fact, like a route to buying that vineyard in Napa one has always dreamed about. The table below reveals the amount of money accumulated over fifty years if one were to invest $52 a year (i.e., $1 a week) into various kinds of investment programs. It makes one's daily cappuccino (cost: $2.75, and that's without a smile) suddenly begin to seem like sheer madness. . . .

Time Horizon	A savings account at a bank[1]	Stocks[2]	Government bonds[3]	Property[4]	Art[5]	Betting on horses[6]	Under the bed
I year	52	52	52	52	52	52	52
2 years	104	107	105	104	105	101	104
3 years	158	166	159	157	159	147	156
4 years	212	229	214	211	215	191	208
5 years	267	295	270	265	272	232	260
10 years	556	702	569	544	579	408	520
25 years	1,567	3,070	1,665	1,468	1753	715	1,300
50 years	3,875	18,118	4,398	3,352	4,925	889	2,600

Note that the big difference in returns really happens between twenty-five and fifty years. The upshot is that skimping on cappuccinos can help one build up a significant nest egg over a long period of time. So if the plan is to move to Napa on retirement, marvelous. However, for those who plan to move there significantly in advance of retirement (i.e., within the next ten years or so), there are various alternative options:

---

1 Assuming that the average real return per annum is 1.5% (sources: www.money.com and others). There are various points, however, to bear in mind: the long-term average always includes all sorts of cycles; the effects of inflation have to be factored in (i.e., with U.S. inflation at about 2.5% at the beginning of 2007, those whose interest rate is claimed by the bank to be, say, 4.5% are actually receiving a real interest return of 2%—in other words, not as great as it sounds); and do not forget that bank interest is taxed, so the real return becomes lower still. All in all, it is a tricky business, and it is these very complexities that keep financial advisers rich and able to pay their children's tuitions.

2 Assuming that the average real return per annum is 6.5% (source: E. Dimson, P. Marsh, and D. Staunton, *Triumph of the Optimists* (2002) as quoted in *ABN AMRO/LBS Global Investment Handbook* (2007). See also Robert Schiller, *The Life-Cycle Personal Accounts Proposal for Social Security: An Evaluation* (2005). Again, there are various points to bear in mind: the transaction costs for stocks and shares tend to be high; the return on

- Very serious saving, at the expense not just of cappuccinos but all sorts of other pleasures

- Earning buckets of money

- Becoming a very skilled or very lucky short-term investor

But beware—history is not, the actuaries now believe, a good guide to the future. The rates quoted above may be an overestimate of what one can now expect. Yields have been coming down (a result of the success of the world economy), creating a crisis for pension funds. In other words, it is a very inexact science unless one is able to see into the future; hence, it is also worth considering completely ignoring all the above suggestions, and going to see an independent financial advisor instead.

---

stocks and shares is made up of the increase in capital value *plus* the dividends; and, finally, most in the financial world are predicting that the real return per annum is likely to fall very soon to more like 5%.

3 Assuming that the average real return per annum is 2% (source: E. Dimson, P. Marsh, and D. Staunton, *Triumph of the Optimists* (2002) as quoted in *ABN AMRO/LBS Global Investment Handbook* (2007). See also the *Wall Street Journal* (Feb. 28, 2005). As with stocks and shares, the transaction costs for treasury bonds tend to be high.

4 Assuming that (in the long term, as ever) the average real return per annum on U.S. residential property is 1% (sources: Schiller and others). Do not be seduced by dinner party chat. Houses, as investments, are not as good as equity. However, since the equity return is made up of the increase in capital value plus the dividends, if one regards living in a house as a dividend then the long-term returns may be roughly the same—that is, quite good.

5 Assuming that the average real return per annum is 2.4% (source: "Accounting for Taste: Art and the Financial Markets over Three Centuries" by W. N. Goetzman in *American Economic Review* Volume 83); but this is contested. Some research suggests that the return is slightly better than equities, and that it has the additional advantage of diversification; others suggest that sale prices are not a true index because they conceal not only high transaction costs, but also all the art that never gets sold (and instead just sits in the attic).

6 Assuming that the average real return per annum is -5.5% (source: Gavyn Davies in the *Guardian*, July 27, 2006, drawing on analysis of 6,301,016 U.S. horse races between 1992 and 2001). Bear in mind, however, that this only applies if one bets just on the favorites; if one bets on the medium favorites (3/1 to 15/1), the return will be closer to -18%.

Sailing

Have no illusions: sailing is not for the delicate of disposition. So before accepting an invitation to spend the day at sea, be sure to find out exactly what sort of trip is planned. Will you be required merely to lounge around in a bikini drinking cocktails, the most pressing matter of the day being which factor sunscreen to use? Or will you be expected to act as a member of the crew?

If the latter, the principal challenge will be to attempt to follow a succession of all but incomprehensible instructions, usually shouted at you through the wind and rain as you slide from one side of the boat to the other, not unlike a flailing puppy. For to bestow upon someone the title of "ship's captain" for the day is to have them morph before your eyes from a calm and rational member of the human race into a ranting lunatic. Tales abound within the sailing community of crew members seen suddenly jumping overboard and swimming to shore with just a single backward glance to yell "I want a divorce" at the ship's captain (a.k.a. the husband), after being shouted at one too many times for having yanked at the main sheet rather than the spinnaker—or whatever. So be warned.

Some other sailing tips include: Pee before embarking. Be sure to take extra hairpins, as well as sunglasses, for within an hour the latter will have fallen off and broken. Hold on tightly. And be patient, even when the trip turns out to last a little longer than expected: Ellen McArthur was at sea for over seventy-one days in order to break the record for the fastest solo nonstop circumnavigation of the world, and even she admits to crying a couple of times.

THE TERMINOLOGY

Fore. Front.

Aft. Back.

Bow. The front of the boat.

Stern. The back of the boat.

Boom. A horizontal pole used to support rigging that threatens to knock a beginner unconscious at any opportunity. Beware.

Port. The left-hand side of the boat when facing forward.

Starboard. The right-hand side of the boat when facing forward.

To tack. To turn the bow of the boat through the wind so that the boat changes direction.

Port tack. The wind is on the port side.

Starboard tack. The wind is on the starboard side.

To jibe (or gybe). To turn the stern of the boat through the wind so that the boat changes direction.

Windward. Toward the wind.

Leeward. Away from the wind.

Stand-on. One's own boat has the right of way, so maintain speed and course.

Give way. The approaching boat has right of way, so alter speed and course to avoid it.

Bulkhead. Wall.

Overheads. Ceiling.

Deck/sole. Floor.

Head. Bathroom.

Galley. Kitchen.

Line. Rope. An ignorance of this one aspect of sailing seems particularly to irritate experienced sailors. It may seem dull, but it is really important. A line means a rope, and onboard each line has a particular purpose. Any that are attached to sails to control their shapes are known as **sheets**; so, for instance, the main sheet is the line that controls the main sail and the spinnaker sheet is the line that controls the spinnaker (the large triangular sail at the front of the boat). A line that raises a sail is a halyard, and one that lowers it is a downhaul or a Cunningham. A line used to tie up the boat is a dock line.

FREQUENTLY HEARD INSTRUCTIONS

These tend to concern modifying the direction of the boat in order to respond to the direction of the wind. If the captain (or whoever is at the helm) shouts "Ready to tack?", the correct response is to shout back with equal gusto, "Ready!" Similarly, "Ready to jibe?" demands a "Ready!" Also crucial to comprehend is "Make fast that line!" which translates as "Tie up that rope!"—an instruction that is particularly welcome when heard near the dock because it usually means that the trip is at an end and a gin and tonic at the sailing club bar is at last within reach.

The Window Box

Nothing transforms the look of a house or an apartment as much as a colorful, blooming window box. Conversely, there is nothing as depressing as the sight of a dead window box. It costs so little, takes so little time and so little effort, and yet can have such a great effect—it is really, really worth doing.

The window box itself should be wooden, lead, or plain earthenware (never plastic). Twice a year, take a trip to a garden center to buy plants and (although you only need to do this once a year) some soil to add to the existing soil—the older, tired-looking stuff needs to be spooned out and replaced with fresh dirt. In September, plant the first bulbs: daffodils are the easiest, while tulips are also worth considering (but see below about going native) as long as there are no squirrels around, in which case forget it. Plant the daffodil or tulip bulbs about two or three inches down; above them and spaced three inches apart in between them, try winter-flowering pansies (all in one color if you want to be truly chic). The difficult part is getting the plants out of the polystyrene containers—a knife helps. The pansies will last for a couple of months, during which time they need to be watered once a week if it does not rain; those who can be bothered may also want to add a teaspoon of liquid fertilizer to the water.

When the pansies have had it, throw them away and replace them with some common box plants (this is a type of plant, by the way, not advice on where to grow it, as the more amateur gardeners among us might suppose—its proper name is *buxus sempervirens*), either on their own or interspersed with red bobbly plants known as winter cherries or *capiscum solanum*.

In the spring, the daffodils will start to come up. When they do, dig up the spent *solanum* and throw them away; it is also worth considering digging up the box plants and moving them elsewhere, it being a bit dull to have evergreens like these all year round. A fallow period then ensues, during which some colored primulas (planted when flowering) are just the thing: they do not last long but are very cheery while they do. These may be planted on top of the daffodil bulbs, which at this stage will also need a bit of attention in the form of some liquid fertilizer if the bulbs are to have any chance of flowering the following year.

May is the month to plant petunias or geraniums. Again, these should all be in the same color. Once a week, you have to pinch off the dead flowers so that new ones grow; but this is actually rather fun and therapeutic and only takes a couple of minutes. They then last until September, when everything but the daffodils should be dug up. The whole cycle then begins again.

A few general points to note are: generally, it does not matter overly much whether the window box is placed in the sun or the shade; everything should be planted fairly close together—two or three inches apart, perhaps; and water once or twice a week unless it rains, in which case, don't bother.

Finally, the fact that there are eleven different planting zones in the continental United States means that everything suggested here will need to be adapted to your local climate. This is not the only reason that, in an ideal world, you should ensure that all the plants chosen for the window box are native to your area.

One of the main reasons for this is that native plants tend to require the least maintenance, adapted as they are already to local soils and climate. In addition, it is important that everyone does his or her part to conserve the United States's flora in the face of so much destruction of the natural environment elsewhere. To this end, consult the native plant database at the website of the Lady Bird Johnson Wildflower Center (www.wildflower.org).

SOME NORTH AMERICAN NATIVE PLANTS
BEGINNING WITH THE LETTER *A*

LATIN NAME	COMMON NAME
Abies amabilis	Pacific silver fir
Abies balsamea	Balsam fir
Abies bracteata	Bristlecone fir
Abies concolor	White fir
Abies fraseri	Fraser fir
Abies grandis	Giant fir
Abies lasiocarpa	Subalpine fir
Abies magnifica	California red fir
Abies procera	Noble fir
Abronia ameliae	Amelia's sand verbena
Abronia angustifolia	Purple sand verbena
Abronia elliptica	Fragrant white sand verbena
Abronia fragrans	Snowball sand verbena
Abronia latifolia	Coastal or yellow sand verbena
Abronia maritima	Red sand verbena
Abronia mellifera	White sand verbena

Latin name	Common name
Abronia pogonantha	Mojave sand verbena
Abronia umbellata	Pink sand verbena
Abronia villosa	Desert sand verbena
Abrus precatorius	Rosary pea
Abutilon fruticosum	Indian mallow
Abutilon hypoleucum	Whiteleaf Indian mallow
Abutilon incanum	Pelotazo
Abutilon parvulum	Dwarf Indian mallow
Acacia angustissima	Prairie acacia/Whiteball acacia
Acacia angustissima var. texensis	Prairie wattle
Acacia berlandieri	Berlandier acacia/Guajillo
Acacia constricta	Whitethorn acacia
Acacia farnesiana	Sweet acacia
Acacia greggii	Catclaw acacia
Acacia neovernicosa	Viscid acacia
Acacia rigidula	Blackbrush acacia
Acacia roemeriana	Roundflower catclaw/Roemer acacia
Acacia schaffneri var. bravoensis	Schaffner's wattle
Acacia tortuosa	Poponax/Huisachillo
Acalypha gracilens	Slender threeseed mercury
Acalypha monococca	Slender threeseed mercury
Acalypha ostryifolia	Pineland threeseed mercury
Acalypha phleoides	Shrubby copperleaf
Acalypha radians	Cardinal's feather
Acalypha rhomboidea	Common threeseed mercury
Acalypha virginica	Virginia threeseed mercury
Acamptopappus shockleyi	Shockley's goldenhead

Latin name	Common name
Acer barbatum	Southern sugar maple
Acer circinatum	Vine maple
Acer glabrum	Rocky Mountain maple
Acer glabrum var. douglasii	Douglas maple
Acer grandidentatum	Bigtooth maple
Acer leucoderme	Chalk maple
Acer macrophyllum	Big-leaf maple
Acer negundo	Ash-leaf maple/Boxelder
Acer nigrum	Black maple
Acer pensylvanicum	Striped maple
Acer rubrum	Red maple
Acer rubrum var. drummondii	Drummond red maple
Acer saccharinum	Silver maple
Acer saccharum	Sugar maple
Acer spicatum	Mountain maple
Achillea millefolium	Common yarrow
Achillea millefolium var. borealis	Boreal yarrow
Achillea millefolium var. occidentalis	Western yarrow
Achillea sibirica	Siberian yarrow
Achlys triphylla	Vanilla leaf/Sweet after death
Achnatherum coronatum	Giant rice grass
Achnatherum hymenoides	Indian rice grass
Achnatherum lettermanii	Letterman's needlegrass
Achnatherum nelsonii ssp. dorei	Dore's needlegrass
Achnatherum richardsonii	Richardson's needlegrass
Achyrachaena mollis	Blow wives
Aceisanthes longiflora	Angel's trumpets
Aceisanthes obtusa	Berlandier's trumpets

Latin name	Common name
Acmella oppositifolia var. repens	Opposite-leaf spotflower
Acoelorraphe wrightii	Everglades palm
Aconitum columbianum	Columbian monkshood
Aconitum delphiniifolium	Larkspur-leaf monkshood
Aconitum noveboracense	Northern blue monkshood
Aconitum uncinatum	Southern blue monkshood
Acorus americanus	Sweetflag
Acorus calamus	Calamus
Acourtia nana	Dwarf desertpeony
Acourtia runcinata	Featherleaf desertpeony
Acourtia thurberi	Thurber's desertpeony
Acourtia wrightii	Brownfoot
Actaea elata	Tall bugbane
Actaea pachypoda	White baneberry
Actaea racemosa var. racemosa	Black bugbane
Actaea rubra	Red baneberry
Adenium obesum	Desert-rose
Adenocaulon bicolor	American trailplant
Adenostoma fasciculatum	Chamise
Adenostoma sparsifolium	Redshank
Adiantum capillus-veneris	Southern maidenhair
Adiantum pedatum	Northern maidenhair
Aesculus californica	California buckeye
Aesculus flava	Sweet buckeye/Yellow buckeye
Aesculus glabra	Ohio buckeye
Aesculus parviflora	Bottlebrush buckeye
Aesculus pavia	Red buckeye
Agalinis edwardsiana	Plateau false foxglove
Agalinis fasciculata	Beach false foxglove

Latin name	Common name
Agalinis gattingeri	Roundstem false foxglove
Agalinis heterophylla	Prairie false foxglove
Agalinis linifolia	Flaxleaf false foxglove
Agalinis maritima	Saltmarsh false foxglove
Agalinis neoscotica	Middleton false foxglove
Agalinis oligophylla	Ridgestem false foxglove
Agalinis paupercula	Smallflower false foxglove
Agalinis purpurea	Purple false foxglove
Agalinis setacea	Threadleaf false foxglove
Agalinis skinneriana	Skinner's false foxglove
Agalinis tenuifolia	Slenderleaf false foxglove
Agarista populifolia	Florida hobblebush
Agastache foeniculum	Blue giant hyssop
Agastache nepetoides	Yellow giant hyssop
Agastache scrophulariifolia	Purple giant hyssop
Agastache urticifolia	Nettleleaf giant hyssop

Philosophy

THE FOUR MAIN STRAINS OF
WESTERN PHILOSOPHY

Ancient Greek philosophy: e.g., Socrates, Plato, Aristotle, Thales, Epicurus

Enlightenment philosophy: e.g., Kant, Hume, Descartes, Spinoza, Locke

Modern analytic philosophy: e.g., Wittgenstein, Russell, Frege, Quine, Rawls

Modern continental philosophy: e.g., Nietzsche, Marx, Sartre, Heidegger, Foucault

The acrimonious split between analytic and continental philosophy happened some time between the early nineteenth century and the early twentieth. It is one of those feuds in which analytic philosophy remains bitter and resentful years later, while continental philosophy is only vaguely aware that analytic philosophy still even exists.

SOME QUESTIONS THAT, CONTRARY TO POPULAR MISCONCEPTION, PHILOSOPHERS RARELY, IF EVER, ASK

What is the meaning of life?

If a tree falls in a forest and there is nobody there to hear it, does it make a sound?

How can I calm down?

NOT TO BE SEATED NEXT TO EACH OTHER AT A DINNER PARTY

A philosopher who has denied the existence of the mind: B.F. Skinner

A philosopher who has denied the existence of anything other than the mind: Plotinus

A philosopher who has denied the existence of God: Friedrich Nietzsche

A philosopher who has denied the existence of anything other than God: George Berkeley

A philosopher who has denied the existence of change: Parmenides

A philosopher who has denied the existence of anything changeless: Heraclitus

FIVE PHILOSOPHY BOOKS THAT CHANGED PHILOSOPHY

1. Plato's *Republic* (ca. 360 B.C.)—posed many of the questions that philosophy has been trying to answer ever since.

2. Aristotle's *Logic* (ca. 350 B.C.)—provided tools for deduction that were not supplanted until the arrival of Gottlieb Frege (see below).

3. René Descartes's *Meditations* (1641)—posited that one can't be sure that anything exists except one's own mind.

4. Hume's *An Enquiry Concerning Human Understanding* (1748)—shattered many assumptions about science and epistemology.

5. Gottlieb Frege's *Begriffsschrift* (1879)—invented the modern system of predicate logic.

FIVE PHILOSOPHY BOOKS THAT CHANGED EVERYTHING ELSE

1. Confucius's *The Analects of Confucius* (ca. 500 B.C.)—advice for living that has been followed in China for centuries.

2. John Locke's *Two Treatises of Government* (1689)—argues for the democratic rights that were later enshrined in the American Constitution.

3. Karl Marx and Friedrich Engels's *The Communist Manifesto* (1848)—a call for revolution across the world.

4. Friedrich Nietzsche's *Beyond Good and Evil* (1886)—influenced everyone from the Nazis to the French Existentialists to The Doors.

5. Peter Singer's *Animal Liberation* (1975)—converted countless people into vegetarian antivivisectionists.

FIVE MOST IMPENETRABLE PHILOSOPHY BOOKS

1. Immanuel Kant's *The Critique of Pure Reason* (1781)—argues that our experience of the world is mediated by mental concepts.

2. Georg Hegel's *The Phenomenology of Spirit* (1807)—explains how human consciousness evolves toward transcendence.

3. Bertrand Russell's *Principia Mathematica* (1913)—attempts to derive the whole of mathematics from logical principles.

4. Ludwig Wittgenstein's *Tractatus Logico-Philosophicus* (1921)—questions the relationship between language and reality.

5. Martin Heidegger's *Being and Time* (1927)—asks why there is something instead of nothing.

FIVE MOST DEPRESSING PHILOSOPHY BOOKS

1. Niccolo Machiavelli's *The Prince* (1532)—argues that the best way to succeed in politics is to be utterly amoral.

2. Thomas Hobbes's *Leviathan* (1651)—argues that society would degenerate into savagery without an oppressive government.

3. Arthur Schopenhauer's *Essays and Aphorisms* (1851)—argues that suffering is an intrinsic part of the human condition.

4. Friedrich Nietzsche's *The Genealogy of Morals* (1887)—argues that the very idea of being nice to others is a ploy by the weak to hold back the strong.

5. Guy Debord's *The Society of the Spectacle* (1967)—argues that everything in life is part of the inescapable hellish circus of capitalism.

FIVE MOST OPTIMISTIC PHILOSOPHY BOOKS

1. Plato's *Meno* (ca. 380 B.C.)—argues that everyone is capable of knowledge and knowledge leads to virtue.

2. Epicurus's *Letters* (ca. 310 B.C.)—"Don't fear God, don't worry about death; what is good is easy to get, and what is terrible is easy to endure."

3. Gottfried Liebniz's *Theodicy* (1710)—claimed (as satirized by Voltaire in *Candide*) that we live in the best of all possible worlds.

4. Georg Hegel's *The Phenomenology of Spirit* (1807)—predicted that humanity would ascend toward the transcendent knowledge that would reconcile us with the world and our own existence.

5. . . . is stretching it. Philosophy by its very nature is not a particularly optimistic pastime.

Toward Helen of Troy

In 2004 Americans spent $12.4 billion on cosmetics. $12.4 billion? It's an awful lot of money, isn't it? One alternative is simply to throw out all the extraneous beauty products that were purchased many moons ago—in the hope they would magically a) make you look like Audrey Hepburn, b) get you a promotion, and c) get you more sex, but that now tend to mope at the back of the medicine cabinet—and gallivant off to a salon for the afternoon instead. Some of the treatments offered at a salon are similarly based on piffle, but at least it is the kind of piffle that allows you to relax for an hour or two without the telephone ringing or the children screeching.

THE BEAUTY SALON

Some women are devoted to the salon; to others, however, it represents a nightmarish world of embarrassment and confusion, in particular when it comes to any kind of full-body treatment like a massage or exfoliation. For those who fall into the latter category, there is one particular conundrum that dominates: Pants or No Pants? 'Tis indeed a tricky one. A good beauty therapist will give clear instructions unprompted, but there are times when such instructions fail to materialize (often when one is abroad), at which point a fallback position is required, which is: If in doubt, keep the Pants on. This applies generally, in fact.

Beauty treatment (y-axis label)

| Pedicure[1] |
| Colonic irrigation[2] |
| Facial waxing (excluding eyebrows)[3] |
| Any all-over body treatment (including scrubs, wraps, and exfoliation)[4] |
| Manicure[5] |
| Facial[6] |
| Leg wax[7] |
| Bikini wax[8] |
| Eyebrow shaping[9] |
| Massage[10] |

Degree of pointlessness

1   No. A pedicure is a waste of time. Life is too short to worry about the way one's feet look.

2   No. So 1990s.

3   No. The benefits are far outweighed by the embarrassment factor.

4   Fine, and very relaxing, but in terms of physical results, unless one has the time and money to do it once a week, more effect can be had from the purchase of a lovely new dress or some excellent underwear. Best left to a girls' weekend away.

5   Yes, for those who live the kind of life whereby a manicure stays intact for more than about ten minutes.

6   Often very beneficial. But is one meant to talk to the therapist while having a facial, or pretend to be asleep? The key is to maintain a delicate state of suspended animation: Do not talk, but at the same time make it clear that one is not asleep, perhaps by clearing one's throat occasionally, or even wriggling slightly.

7   Yes, especially for vacations when one has far better things to do of a bright, sparkling morning than spend an extra five minutes in the shower wrestling with a razor.

8   Yes, in moderation.

9   Makes all the difference. But beware of women with overly thin eyebrows. They are not to be trusted.

10   Yes please. Note, however, that a "couple's massage" is never advisable as they are the very opposite of relaxing. Is one supposed to chat? Not chat? Look at each other? Not look at each other? It invariably leads to an uncontrollable giggling fit, and hence a perturbed, sometimes offended, massage therapist. Avoid.

How to Get Rid of Guests at the End of a Dinner Party

While much has been written on the subject of receiving guests into one's home, there is, alas, precious little advice available on the subject of ejecting them. The dinner parties of today have the natural advantage of tending to take place in the evening, by which point many are already beginning to ponder the various pleasures that going home and crawling into bed hold. This was not always the case. In the Middle Ages, dinner was eaten at around one o'clock, and it was only with the stirrings of industrialization that the main meal of the day began to shift ever later—to three o'clock in the 1730s, five o'clock in the 1770s, seven o'clock in the 1800s and nine o'clock in the 1840s, a time around which it has fluctuated, by an hour or so each way, ever since. However, should the sheer lateness of the hour fail to persuade the assembled guests that it is time to wend their merry ways home, here is a selection of techniques designed to precipitate their departure, while causing minimum offense:

1. Do not supply guests with any stimulants, legal or otherwise, as this will only prolong the agony—the likes of coffee should be eschewed in favor of chamomile tea.

2. If conversation should reach a natural lull, do not attempt to reignite it.

3. Subtly cease refilling wineglasses and on no account open new bottles of anything.

4. Start clearing the table and guests are very likely to leave—if only to avoid assisting in the cleaning up.

5. Take a tip from bar owners and make the surroundings subliminally less agreeable: brighten the lights; allow the room to become chilly by opening a window; put some challenging music on the gramophone.

6. Once on your feet, remain standing; lingering by the door will politely suggest that it is time to go.

7. As a last resort, feign an altercation between you and your fellow host: an unseemly domestic incident will rid you of unwanted guests in a speedier fashion than anything else.

American Literature over the Past Three Hundred and Fifty Years

Just because a book is new does not mean it is any more worthy of our attention than many of the thousands of books published one hundred, two hundred, or even three hundred and fifty years ago. Often, quite the opposite is true. With this in mind, below is a highly selective and unauthoritative list of some of the most notable, laudable, or just downright eccentric American literature published over the past three centuries or so.

Year	Title	Author
1657	The Watering of the Olive Plant in Christs Garden	John Fiske
	The Application of Redemption	Thomas Hooker

Year	Title	Author
	A Farewell Exhortation to the Church and People of Dorchester in New England	Richard Mather
1707	*A Poem on Elijah's Translation, occasioned by the death of Rev. Samuel Willard*	Benjamin Colman
	A Practical Discourse on the Parable of the Ten Virgins	Benjamin Colman
	A Narrative of a New and Unusual American Imprisonment	Francis Makemie
	A Memorial of the Present Deplorable State of New-England	Cotton Mather
	Manly Christianity: A Brief Essay on the Sighs of Growth and Strength in the most Lovely Christianity	Cotton Mather
	The Redeemed Captive	John Williams[1]
1757	*Poems on Divers Subjects*	Martha Wadsworth Brewster[2]
	The Choice	Benjamin Church
1807	*Tears and Smiles*	James Nelson Barker
	The Columbiad	Joel Barlow
	Ira and Isabella; or, The Natural Children	William Hill Brown
	The Battle of Eutaw Springs	William Ioor

---

1   A best-selling account of being held in captivity in Canada for two and a half years, first by Abenaki Indians and then by the French. Williams was the pastor of the Congregational church in Deerfield, Massachusetts when (as his tale begins) "On Tuesday the 29th of February, 1703–4, not long before break of day, the enemy came in like a flood upon us; our watch being unfaithful: an evil, whose awful effects, in a surprizal of our fort, should bespeak all watchmen to avoid, as they would not bring the charge of blood upon themselves. . . ."

2   One of only four books of poetry by a woman ever published in colonial America.

Year	Title	Author
	Salmagundi; or, The Whim-Whams and Opinions of Launcelot Langstaff, Esq., and Others	Washington Irving
	Margaretta; or, The Intricacies of the Heart	Martha Meredith Read
1857	*Contributions to the Natural History of the United States*	Jean Louis Rodolphe Agassiz
	The Philosophy of the Plays of Shakespeare Unfolded	Delia Bacon
	Abridgment of the Debates of Congress from 1789 to 1856	Thomas Hart Benton
	The Poor of New York	Dion Boucicault
	Love in '76	Oliver Bell Bunce
	Nothing to Wear	William Allen Butler
	Autobiography of Peter Cartwright, the Backwoods Preacher	Peter Cartwright
	Thanksgiving Day	Lydia Maria Child
	Mabel Vuaghan	Maria Susanna Cummins
	The Impending Crisis of the South: How to Meet It	Hinton Rowan Helper
	The World's Own	Julia Ward Howe
	The Hasheesh eater	Fitz Hugh Ludlow
	The Confidence-Man: His Masquerade	Herman Melville
	The Life and Times of Aaron Burr	James Parton
	Married or Single?	Catharine Maria Sedgwick[3]

---

3 One of the most popular novelists of the era, Sedgwick's subject matter tended to be domestic, but also feminist, in theme. As she writes in the introduction to *Married or Single*, ". . . we raise our voice with all our might against the miserable cant that matrimony is essential to the feebler sex—that a woman's single life must be useless or undignified—that she is but an

Year	Title	Author
	Neighbor Jackwood	John Townsend Trowbridge
	The Garies and Their Friends	Frank J. Webb
	Paul Fane; or, Parts of a Life Else Untold	Nathaniel Parker Willis
1907	*The Education of Henry Adams*	Henry Adams
	The Truth	Clyde Fitch
	The Trimmed Lamp	O. Henry (William Sydney Porter)
	The American Scene	Henry James
	The High Bid	Henry James
	Pragmatism: A New Name for Some Old Ways of Thinking	William James
	The Road	Jack London
	Love of Life and Other Stories	Jack London
	Polly of the Circus	Margaret Mayo
	The Red City: A Novel of the Second Administration of President Washington	S. Weir Mitchell
	The Lonesome Trail	John G. Neihardt
	Folkways	William Graham Sumner
	The Witching Hour	Augustus Thomas
	Christian Science	Mark Twain
	Madame de Treymes	Edith Wharton[4]
	The Fruit of the Tree	Edith Wharton
	The Turn of the Balance	Brand Whitlock

adjunct of man—in her best estate a helm merely to guide the nobler vessel. Aside from the great tasks of humanity, for which masculine capacities are best fitted, we believe she has an independent power to shape her own course, and to force her separate sovereign way." Radical indeed.

4   This was Wharton's first book after moving to Paris, so it is not surprising that one of its major themes is the cultural differences between the Americans and the French. Also worth noting is the unsurpassable name of the book's heroine: Franny Frisbee.

Year	Title	Author
	The Shepherd of the Hills	Harold Bell Wright
1957	*A Death in the Family*	James Agee
	Odd Girl Out	Ann Bannon[5]
	First Love and Other Stories	Harold Brodkey
	The Wapshot Chronicle	John Cheever
	Syntactic Structures	Noam Chomsky
	By Love Possessed	James Gould Cozzens
	The Ordeal of Mansart	W.E.B. Du Bois
	On Poetry and Poets	T.S. Eliot
	The Town	William Faulkner
	A Theory of Cognitive Dissonance	Leon Festinger
	For Love of Imabelle	Chester Himes
	Politics and the Novel	Irving Howe
	Some Come Running	James Jones
	On the Road	Jack Kerouac
	Please Don't Eat the Daisies	Jean Kerr[6]
	West Side Story	Arthur Laurents
	The Flower Drum Song	C.Y. Lee
	The Assistant	Bernard Malamud
	Memoirs of a Catholic Girlhood	Mary McCarthy
	Big Sur and the Oranges of Hieronymus Bosch	Henry Miller
	Love Among the Cannibals	Wright Morris
	Pnin	Vladimir Nabakov
	The Homecoming Game	Howard Nemerov
	A Moon for the Misbegotten	Eugene O'Neill

---

5   The first in a new genre of lesbian pulp fiction. The plot revolves around a lesbian relationship between two college roommates at a midwestern university. It was the second-best selling--paperback of the year.

6   An account of life in the suburbs by a housewife and mother of four young sons. Brilliantly funny, it also boasts one of the most fabulous titles for a book ever conceived.

YEAR	TITLE	AUTHOR
	No-No Boy	John Okada
	The Hidden Persuaders	Vance Packard
	Atlas Shrugged	Ayn Rand
	The Hunters	James Salter
	The Short Reign of Pippin IV	John Steinbeck
	Opus Posthumous	Wallace Stevens
	Visit to a Small Planet	Gore Vidal
	Promises: Poems 1954–1956	Robert Penn Warren
	Orpheus Descending	Tennessee Williams

The Origin of "Woman"

To ascertain the origin of the word "woman," begin with the origins of the word "man," with regards to which a variety of theories exist. "Man" may derive from the Latin word *manus* (hand), or from the Latin root *mens* (mind). It is more likely, however, that it was inspired by a god known as Mannus who was worshipped by various ancient Germanic tribes. Whatever the truth, it is clear that "man" originally referred to a human being of either sex. In other words, our early ancestors were in no way trying to make some kind of sexist statement.

"Man" tended to function as a single syllable within a compound word. The Old English word for woman was *wifman*, where *wif* was a collective plural noun meaning "a family belonging to a woman" or "womankind." (In a similar construction, the Old English word for man was *wæpnedman*, where *wæpned* meant "armed" or "possessing weapons.") The development of *wifman* into *woman* was then a slow, gradual process subject to a number of practical considerations—among them the fact that even once *wifman* had been shortened to *wuman*, this was found to be impractical in the context of medieval script where the letter *w* was written as a double *u*. The result was that *wu* effectively appeared as a triple *u*, making the text not only tricky to read, but also in all likelihood raising (erroneous) concerns that the scribe had not been concentrating quite as closely as perhaps he should have been. Eventually the *u* became an *o* and *wuman* became *woman*. Elements of the word's etymology are evident today: the first syllable of the plural form of the word, "women," has retained the pronunciation of the earlier form of the word, *wifman*, even though the singular form, "woman," has stuck with the later one.

Similarly, the word "girl" has non—gender-specific origins and meant, simply, "a child"—the root is *gir*, which is Scandinavian, with the final *l* a diminutive suffix. "Lass" comes from "rag"; "wench" from "an unsteady one"; "Queen" possibly from the Gothic word *quean*, meaning "woman," though some sources relate it to the Old English word *cwene*, "prostitute."

Finally, let's delight in "daisy," which derives from the Old English phrase *dæges eage*, meaning "day's eye." Is this because the flower resembles the sun? Because the petals close over the yellow "eye" at night, only to open again once morning comes? Who knows? As Plato put it: "The namegiver is the rarest of craftsmen."

Printed in the United States
By Bookmasters